Short Cuts

SHORTCUTS

The Screenplay

Robert Altman *&* Frank Barhydt

PORTRAITS BY

Don Bachardy

Don Bachardy

BASED ON THE STORIES OF

Raymond Carver

CAPRA PRESS

SANTA BARBARA

1993

Cover design by Denise Eltinge.
Book design & typography by Jim Cook.

LIBRARY OF CONGRESS CATALOGING-IN-PUBLICATION DATA
Altman, Robert. 1925–
Short cuts: a screenplay / Robert Altman and Frank Barhydt;
based on the writings of Raymond Carver; with portraits by Don Bachardy.
p.   cm.
ISBN 0-88496-378-0: $16.95
I. Barhydt, Frank. II. Carver, Raymond. Short cuts. III. Title
997.S477A48   1993
791.43'72—dc20   93-4437
CIP

CAPRA PRESS
Post Office Box 2068
Santa Barbara, CA 93120

CONTENTS

Foreword

TESS GALLAGHER

Robert Altman sits next to me on the bed with Anne Archer in her cotton nightie squeezed against him, his hand balancing at her waist. She readies herself as "Claire" to cross to the bathroom where she will speak back toward Fred Ward (Stuart) from the *Short Cuts* script.

By then I've read the script in at least two different versions. Before that I'd seen revisions and published versions of the story, "So Much Water So Close to Home" by Raymond Carver, on which this scene had been based. In its final form it had appeared in Ray's last collection *Where I'm Calling From*.

The reverberation of this current connecting Ray's writing with the script by Altman and Barhydt, passing into these flesh and blood characters being fixed on celluloid has begun, in the cramped space of that room, to cause my molecules to chatter and collide. I hope it isn't audible because the half-threat call of "Rolling!" has already gone out and Walt Lloyd, the cinematographer, is bent to the camera. *Film is rolling.*

There is a vibrant calm at the center of fire. This is the calm I entered in the unbearable heat of the tiny bedroom of Claire and Stuart on location for *Short Cuts* as it was being shot in L.A. in August of 1992.

Someone had cut the power to the motorized, body-thick duct of cool air that had been shushing into the space through a second story window. At dawn the house had been cloaked in black tarp to shoot these night scenes. *The camera is rolling.* It is the quiet of unfinished arguments, of Mafia hats at dawn—the air impending and alert. But what a population looks on! Members of the crew hover unobtrusively in doorways and crannies, crouched and leaning in the stairwell, stilled like children in a game of statues on a postage stamp-sized lawn.

Claire looks back at her husband, Stuart, who's just told her that for three days and nights he'd left a woman's body tied in a river while he fished with his friends. *The camera is rolling.* Claire's expression of bafflement shifts into slow but steady disbelief in the icy flicker of the monitor which shows what the cam-

7

era is picking up. Her face seems enormous like anything newborn because, I suppose, of that special amplification time takes on when you know its images are being preserved.

The moments I was living had been a long while arriving, it seemed. All the way back to a newspaper article which had sparked Ray's story, forward to Frank Barhydt's sister giving him a book by Carver in 1988, the year Ray died, and then to Altman on a plane coming home from Italy, reading Carver stories as aftermath to his own changed direction.

The curious thing too was that even with all the import of filming I've just described, there was also a casualness about what movement did take place around the shooting. Casualness and ease. Someone, something or several someones were in control. Everything was going to happen the best it could and if things went wrong, there would be a way to handle it, even to use slippage to advantage. This agility of spirit Altman brings to his work seemed to free everyone to do their best. I was to appreciate the consistency of that spirit during the numerous visits I would make to the filming locations in August and October.

* * *

There is a feeling of brine and high seas about Robert Altman. He's scow and schooner, scrappy and tested. In stature his 6' 2", his love-to-eat heft, uncannily reminded me of Ray. Directing, he's like a genial, no-nonsense captain with a tender, flexible grip on things, even though he seems to be relying on everyone else present to do exactly what needs to be done, largely without him. When he does speak, it's calmly, as if he's teasing things out, yet with an exactitude rooted deep in the heart of the action as it's evolving from the script. But he's most live to what's coming through the actors in that moment of shooting.

This exploding yet controlled time of the camera-rolling which I've tried to describe would have been sheer chaos without the firm scaffolding of this fine script, initially drafted by Frank Barhydt, a lean, down-to-earth man who laughs easily and whose laconic manner is quietly disarming. Having met him first on the page in his work on the script, I knew myself to be in the company of an impressive writer on his own ground. He also understood the way Ray's characters thought because he had down how they talked. I liked it that in person he didn't seem to need to prove anything to anyone. His relationship to Altman goes back through his own father who'd been Altman's boss in some past era. Barhydt has also worked on three previous projects with Altman.

After discussions with Altman, Frank had roughed out the *Short Cuts* script. Then they put Carver's books aside for the next phase. Over the following months, Altman and Barhydt began to eat, sleep and live Carver's world in its essences, imagining how it could find new life in film and in the things they each had to offer. Frank's Missouri-tanged voice picks up color and velocity remembering how they worked, the way their ideas began to feed into each other out of Carver, so that in the end, it's hard to remember who gave what.

The two would perform variations like jazz musicians on the Carver stories, inventing their own characters to add to his, getting scenes onto colored note cards that let them visualize the wide mosaic on the wall behind them at the intial production office in Malibu. Once, on the phone, Bob and I had talked about how scenes could go more than one way. The scripting of the stories began to reflect this variability of direction. I mentioned to Bob in a follow-up letter that such exploration was deep in the spirit of poetry, all the way back to Aristotle who says poetry deals with "a kind of thing which might happen, i.e. what is possible."

But behind, under and inside this script remain the nine short stories and one poem, "Lemonade," of Raymond Carver. His clarity and precision, the elisions of his characters' speech, the ways they glance off each other in conversation, bruise, circle, plead, lie or seek to persuade are unmistakably carried forward from Carver. As Frank is quick to acknowledge, much of Carver's dialogue was just too good not to use. But it couldn't simply carry at other times either. Film, as Frank puts it, is "wordier." Sometimes an action demands two lines in film where one serves on the page. Sometimes a written thought or attitude will take a series of actions to translate onto film.

Besides the collateral of Carver's wonderful ear for the spoken word as it carries the unspoken, the script also had the charged fabric of Carver's world in which those life verities one depends on might at any instant give way. Altman and Carver probably join at this strange hinge "luck", both of them chancers and creators willing to stake their lives, artistic and otherwise, on the precarious rim of possibility. They've known the dive and swoop of fortune which takes us a step beyond mere courage to that helpless place we all hit at some point where we realize anything could and does happen, and to us.

What I keep admiring in this film script is the way the stories more than coexist. The failure of so many scripts of Carver stories by others I'd seen prior to the Altman/Barhydt project had been to stay so close to the originals that a robotic pandering to the text resulted. They were like someone ice skating with an osprey's egg on which the bird is still nesting. Nothing new came to the stories and they were damp with poignant silences.

Altman and Barhydt broke the frames on the stories and allowed the characters to affect each other's worlds or not, as if to suggest that we are both more "in this together" *and* alone than we ever suspected. There is a high element of surprise and delight simply in re-meeting the characters *Nashville*-style in unexpected conformations. These interactions move Carver into new territory. Often it seems Altman and Barhydt are using Carver to cue what might have been said or done, but was under the surface in the stories.

The trick in this scripting is, of course, to give enough of the unsaid while somehow communicating Carver's gaps and darkness. The shuttle motion of picking up and dropping stories at intervals is one mechanism the film uses to suspend us in its current, then allow us to reapproach what's going on down river.

In early March of 1991 I'd sent Bob five pages of notes, what I called a "champagne read" of the first script I'd seen. I would later send "hard read" notes. But early on I was simply cheerleading. The caliber of that initial script verified my early joy at Altman's having undertaken to use Ray's stories in a film. I could see that he and Barhydt honored the spirit of Ray's work, knew how to give its Kafkaesque "gay and empty ride", its shadows as well as that Chekhovian side Ray came to in the last seven years. I'd read the scenes with what I called "dead-alive eyes", meaning I'd tried to let Ray, as I'd experienced him in our own collaborations, look through. I'd felt how amazed Ray would have been to meet his stories interwoven on one huge canvas in this extraordinary script.

Early on I'd realized that literary widows can get sickeningly nostalgic with 'he would haves.' So I ration that assumptive verb tense. Nonetheless, it serves honestly when I think how much Raymond Carver truly *would have* hated missing the glow and sweep of what has gone forward in the evolution of this scripting. It has passed from his stories to Bob and Frank, to the contributions of the crew, the inspiration of the actors, then into the cutting room and now into theaters around the world, embraced and chastened, galvanized and amplified, reinterpreted by the many-headed hydra of collaborative intensity which is filmmaking—admittedly a galaxy away from the solitude in which Ray's writing was accomplished. But Ray was a realist who knew the difference between the action of the hive and of the cleaver. This scripting is amazing for how it orchestrates for both.

Risking trespass, I will say I believe Ray's attitude toward Altman's use of his work would have been one of permission to an artist of equal stature. Ray's capacity for delight is legendary. He surrendered to those things he loved. He was a straight-on admirer of Robert Altman, whose *Nashville* we'd watched more than once on video together and considered one of the most inspired, patently American films yet made.

Ray would have shown a generous curiosity about the new shape his stories would inevitably take. I imagine him exuberant at the dailies, swilling lemonade, laughing with his whole body at his smaller violences of snipped telephone cords becoming larger, more surgically destructive in Stormy Weather's chain saw massacre of his wife's living room furniture. He would appreciate the shifting of emphasis in Altman's version of "So Much Water So Close to Home"—how he uncovers something about the differences between the sexes by being more even-handed with blame in a story which belonged firmly in Carver to the dilemmas of its women.

Altman and Barhydt both have a great sense of the dryly comic and they've brought to the surface Carver's own willingness to laugh with, not at, his characters. The most cautionary advice I gave Bob was the sense that Ray never raised himself above the plights of his characters. He was nose-to-nose with them, feeling the ruptures in intimacy and coherence which split their lives apart. This was to hint at restraining one of Bob's most potent and incisive artistic tools—irony. I typed up and gave him lines from Rainer Maria Rilke's *Letters to a Young Poet* which, while admitting that irony "cleanly used is also clean" advises that one "shouldn't be governed by it . . . Seek the depth of things: thither irony never descends. . . "

While such advice smacks perhaps of the confinements of the literary, it is also true that irony, in the more public mediums of television and film, often becomes the contemporary escape hatch to avoid genuine feeling. Ray's story "A Small, Good Thing" would have set Bob's compass in this regard if I'd said nothing. Because it centers around the death of a child, it required and got Bob's consummate skill in keeping the depth, yet not tipping into sentimentality or drawing away from the emotions. It is the story left most intact by the scripting, and, along with the Jack Lemmon portrait of the adulterous father, it is one of the places the film lets the suffering of the characters open out most—hands and heart on.

Altman's difference from Carver is that he often shifts the cries of the characters into the wider arena of the audience by withholding them on screen. For instance in a Carver story like "Jerry and Molly and Sam" the adulterous husband silently asks himself "Is there a chance for me?" But in Altman we see Gene retrieve the family dog he's abandoned, then return home as if he's never betrayed anyone—though he has, and the fact that the audience knows it serves as the inner ache he is too compulsive even to acknowledge.

Carver's characters grapple with their fates in the matter-of-fact voices of his narrators, but in film this all has to happen as action, not introspection. The effect of this necessary translation is at times to toughen and speed up what is tender and circuitous in Carver. Altman and Barhydt's intuitive feel for the need to restore tenderness can be felt in moments of vulnerability with characters like Doreen Piggott, the waitress played by Lily Tomlin, when she runs after the child she's hit with her car, pleading with him to let her take him home—realizing aloud to her husband (Tom Waits) later, then to her daughter (Lili Taylor) that her whole life could have changed if the child had been killed. The audience must bridge this near-escape to bear the truth—that the child *does* in fact die. Doreen's ignorance of this caresses the audience's pain register each time she repeats how close she came to killing the child.

With Altman we can't escape the steepness of the ravine rushing up at us. If Carver fans miss the redemptive interior voices of his baffled Middle-American characters in the film, it's because in the stories these brief glimpses of their hopes being blunted by realities do serve to cushion our fall.

I'm reminded of a remark by Pablo Neruda's friend Roberto Matta: "One has to be in despair about everything, in order to defeat despair." This hard assignment—to feel the pervasiveness of the American malaise—seems crucial to Altman and Barhydt's revisioning of Carver. The film audience, to a large extent, becomes its own interior narrator, a dazed character eventually forced outside the theater who keeps ruminating the half-articulated, glancing-off pain they've just witnessed.

Both stories and film use the whole keyboard of human proclivities, but the film is huge with appetite, and because it combines and interlocks stories, it has a ricochet power which the individual stories alone don't carry. There are the reverberating themes of infidelity, denial, sexual exploitation, the alcoholic merry-go-round, irrevocable loss in the death of a child, anonymous and grotesque death in the neglect of the woman's body in "So Much Water So Close to Home," and the disappearance of certain characters into fantasy.

* * *

Throughout the film there is a current of frustrated sexuality which erupts as violence against things and other people, and against the self. Even children coexist in half-deaf innocence within the perverse adult life around them. The circuitry of the film connects these behaviors and themes to each other rather more prismatically than one encounters them in Carver's individual stories.

Good films and good stories raise important questions. This film questions, among other things, women's complicity in their misuse as sexual playthings in the American imagination. They are seen as compliant with the American male need for an anonymity of sexual access to them. The victim-oriented feminism of the 1960s tended to place blame with the patriarchy for what happened to women in their sexual roles and lives. It largely avoided their own acquiescence to what was being done with their images. It knows better now. In this respect and others Altman rather updates Carver to the 90s. I think the film definitely sees men and women in a dangerous partnership in these matters, and this is going to provoke a lot of discussion as to whether the presentation is a distortion, a magnification or whether it reveals that women do in fact often contribute to sexual usury in their wish to be loved at any cost.

There is also a kind of checked-out, matter-of-factness regarding sex, say, in the character of Lois Kaiser (Jennifer Jason Leigh) talking sex on the phone while she diapers her kids. Her character seems to acknowledge that this lack of intimacy is what some men need and that it isn't any big deal to supply it. Especially when it's an easy way to earn a buck and you don't have to see what you do! After all, it's just imagined—right?

In Altman's vision throughout, the connective tissue in American life between what is imagined and what is real is being severed. The emasculation of Lois Kaiser's husband (Christopher Penn) is very compellingly delivered. The moment in the written script when Jerry Kaiser kills the woman with a stone had made me wonder if this action could really credibly be brought off. It had taken many drafts from Ray even to get it to work in the story. As it turned out, I was shocked in viewing the film that, unlike in the Carver story "Tell the Woman We're Going", I could not simply stand in a place of judgment during one of the most violent moments of the film. Altman makes us scarily complicitous.

Altman and Barhydt's scripting keeps the calamitous momentum of action up all the way to the end by scooping up the characters in their separate quiverings in an earthquake. This is a step past the mock, symphonic finale of Nashville. The blues singing of Annie Ross as the widow Tess, played off the cello-undertow of Lori Singer, is also an Altman/Barhydt addition to Carver which joins the stories seamlessly from the inside in a purgatorial world which is probably franker, even more lost than Carver's—and therefore more anguished for its unattended wounds. Tess sings "To Hell with Love" to answer Carver's "What We Talk About When We Talk About Love"—for her, the talking is so over it's raw utterance and rasping good riddance. Such dialogue between Carver and Altman/Barhydt is provocatively alive throughout the script. We have to ask ourselves: what is it we've left behind if, with Tess, we say "to hell with love."

* * *

When, at last, in January of 1993 the film was assembled in its bladder-breaking three-hour-and-ten-minute version in the cutting room in NYC, Altman held a special showing for me. There were celebrities attending, but I wasn't able to spot most of them without cueing from my photographer friend, Marion Ettlinger. (I did recognize and meet Lauren Bacall in the elevator!) All the better to focus on Altman and the film with the lively ghost of Ray beaming in on me.

The fan of images was projected in that small crowded viewing room. Time again slipped out of itself. The jigsaw tapestry of the lives on the screen began to intersect with my own, to make a kind of earthquake in my solar plexus. I was absorbed, hypnotized by the spectacle. It was as if the film compelled its audience to recognize its own deceits, betrayals, exposures and abandonments as Altman recreates them from Carver and adds his own. By the end, the beautiful flawed confusion of human lives had worked its spell on me. Yet it was beyond spell, out into that territory which John Updike says demands "great natural health" in which we are asked to sustain life without illusions.

There was a pervasive sadness and loneliness in the room when the film ended. But also a palpable exhilaration that comes from having been through something large and inexplicable, more achingly comfortless than anyone had guessed they'd have the stamina and will to experience. But we had. We'd come through. When the lights went up we belonged to that world, the fusion of Altman-Carver, made visceral on film—naked, obsessive, rawly innocent, chaotic. It was a poetry of the impure, as if we could suddenly see ourselves worn away by the acid of not knowing what's happening to us as we do what we do, the poetry of food stains and shocks, doubts and stupidities, of loneliness and pirated rooms, injured sex, clingings over hospital beds, splinters of glassy hearts in the freshly vacuumed carpet.

It was natural in aftermath at the restaurant to want to talk about hope, that elusive Carver manna heaven is always intending to drop. Had Altman inscribed our brows with William the Silent's "One need not hope to undertake"? Were we cut off as a people from our pain and suffering because we don't know how or what to hope for anymore? Whatever the intricacies of the diagnosis, we felt the images of the film challenging us.

Art as distinct from the purely entertaining isn't obliged to provide the antidote for its revealed poisons. Ray also had to fight this notion from readers and critics—that the artist was suppose to do more than diagnose the condition of its characters—that he or she was also supposed to rise like the Statue of Liberty on the horizon with some sort of redemptive light.

But in Altman's film, as with Ray's stories, the questions *are* the redemption. What we do with our recognitions, once we gaze into their harsh and tender mirrors, is really on our own ground, outside both the stories and the film. That's the provocative nature of art itself. It says what *is*, as honestly and truly as it can envision it. On this count both Altman and Carver are relentlessly true. They both reach these truths lyrically. Altman's lyricism works by dislocating the narrative, by jump-starting it, by allowing it to love its lost causes even as it leapfrogs them onto the wet cement of the next enormous instant.

On one of my last nights in L.A. at a meal at the Granita restaurant, Altman and I had been talking about our mutual fascination with doubles, the wild probability of gaining that extra likeness which might extend your life into the secret fruitfulness of the path not taken. "Ray was a Gemini," I told Bob, in my by now habitual reflex of keeping Ray present in our conversations. We also spoke about poetry—Ray's love of it. I said I felt Ray's stories had the hum and leap of poetry inside them. Later, as we left the restaurant, Bob came back from the car to where I was standing with Frank at the curbside to plant a kiss on my mouth so firmly it was brotherly. "Goodnight, Poet," he said, and, without a beat I answered: "Goodnight, Other Poet." Thinking double.

SHORTCUTS

FINE LINE FEATURES Presents

In association with
SPELLING FILMS INTERNATIONAL

A CARY BROKAW/AVENUE PICTURES Production

A ROBERT ALTMAN Film

SHORT CUTS

ANDIE MacDOWELL · BRUCE DAVISON

JULIANNE MOORE · MATTHEW MODINE

ANNE ARCHER · FRED WARD

JENNIFER JASON LEIGH · CHRIS PENN

LILI TAYLOR · ROBERT DOWNEY, JR.

MADELEINE STOWE · TIM ROBBINS

LILY TOMLIN · TOM WAITS

FRANCES McDORMAND · PETER GALLAGHER

ANNIE ROSS · LORI SINGER

JACK LEMMON · LYLE LOVETT

BUCK HENRY · HUEY LEWIS

Music Produced by	Hal Willner
Original Score Composed by	Mark Isham
Costumes by	John Hay
Production Designer	Stephen Altman
Edited by	Geraldine Peroni
Director of Photography	Walt Lloyd
Executive Producer	Scott Bushnell
Based on the writings of	Raymond Carver
Screenplay by	Robert Altman & Frank Barhydt
Produced by	Cary Brokaw
Directed by	Robert Altman

SHORTCUTS

FADE IN:
EXT—SCENIC VIEW—NIGHT

A view of the city lights. The sound of helicopters can be heard. The CAMERA PANS RIGHT to reveal a sign illuminated by the helicopter lights: REMEMBER MEDFLY QUARANTINE. The sign vibrates wildly. Looking up we see the helicopters coming in low and spraying Malathion, an insecticide. The sign like everything else gets coated. Then the sign goes dark and the rumble subsides as the last helicopter passes. The CAMERA PANS LEFT to its original view of the twinkling lights. (The MAIN TITLES begin and continue throughout this sequence.)

EXT—SKY OVER L.A.—NIGHT

*FIVE helicopters fly over city in formation spraying Malathion.
CAMERA PANS off the helicopters to a white stretch limousine that is cruising along. It happens to be the only car on the road.*

INT—LIMOUSINE—NIGHT

The TV is on in the back of the limousine. An editorial by HOWARD FINNIGAN discusses the war on the Medfly. EARL PIGGOT, the driver, turns and looks into the back seat. A MAN in a tuxedo, with a stethoscope around his neck, is snuggled up with a YOUNG WOMAN. Both are passed out. EARL takes a drink from a bottle of vodka—the size served by airlines.

EXT—SKY OVER L.A.—NIGHT

As the helicopters continue their mission over the city we hear HOWARD FINNIGAN's editorial. (The editorial is spread out over the first night's scenes.)

EXT—FINNIGAN HOUSE—NIGHT

CAMERA tilts from the dark sky to the Finnigan house. We see a light in the upstairs window. As the CAMERA MOVES IN on the lighted window we hear:

HOWARD: Honey, it's on.

INT—FINNIGAN HOUSE/BEDROOM—NIGHT

HOWARD FINNIGAN'S *editorial continues. From another room we hear* ANN FINNIGAN *answer.*

ANN: Okay I'm coming.

HOWARD *is sitting in bed watching himself on TV.* ANN *comes into the room picks up a stack of catalogues. She climbs into bed beside him.* HOWARD *is concentrating on himself.*

ANN: Do you have to wear the glasses on TV?
HOWARD: Shhhhh.

ANN *opens a catalogue and begins browsing.*

EXT—L.A. SKYLINE—NIGHT

The helicopters fly in formation over the city.

INT—CONCERT HALL—NIGHT

ZOE TRAINER *and the TROUT QUINTET perform VICTOR HERBERT CONCERTO #2.* CLAIRE *and* STUART KANE *are watching the concert. Seated next to them are* MARIAN *and* RALPH WYMAN. MARIAN'S *attention strays from quintet to audience.* RALPH *doesn't like it.*

RALPH: Marian, what's so interesting?

MARIAN *leans towards* CLAIRE.

MARIAN: Isn't that Alex Trebek?

CLAIRE *looks.* STUART *looks to see what she's looking at.*

CLAIRE: Alex Trebek? Where?
MARIAN: Over there. Next to the woman with the white hair.
CLAIRE: Is that Alex Trebek?
MARIAN: Yes. I'm sure it is.
STUART: Who's Alex Trebek?

MARIAN *turns to have another look.* RALPH *is annoyed.*

RALPH: Marian, please.

EXT—KAISER HOUSE—NIGHT

We hear the sound of helicopters as JERRY KAISER *covers up his JERRY'S COOL POOL SERVICE truck with a tarp. He starts towards the house picking up toys from the lawn. He flings them on the front porch.*

INT—KAISER HOUSE—NIGHT

JERRY *can hear his wife* LOIS *talking on the telephone. It sounds like she's talking to another man. The* KAISER *children,* JOE, *7, and* JOSETTE, *a toddler, are present.* HOWARD FINNIGAN'S *editorial continues in the background.*

LOIS: Oh, Andy, you're a long ways away. I'm in L.A.

LOIS *saunters into the living room with a plate of cookies for* JOE. *Her voice is very sexy.*

LOIS: Hear the helicopters?

JERRY *listens to* LOIS. *Then he sits by* JOE. LOIS *starts back into the dining room where* JOSETTE *sits in her highchair.*

LOIS: What are you wearing? Already. That was fast.

EXT—L.A. SKYLINE—NIGHT

The helicopters fly in formation over the city. CAMERA PANS DOWN to a brightly lit 24-HOUR CAFE.

EXT/INT—24-HOUR CAFE—NIGHT

From inside the restaurant we see EARL PIGGOT'S *limo pull into a parking spot.* EARL *gets out, locks the door, then runs a finger across the roof which is covered with the sticky glaze sprayed from the helicopters. He lights a cigarette.* DOREEN PIGGOT, EARL'S *wife and a waitress, is finishing up with the* 400 POUND MAN. EARL *gives her apron string a tug as he passes behind her. She knows it's him.*

DOREEN: Can I get you anything else?

The 400 POUND MAN *shakes his head.* DOREEN *walks to the counter where* EARL *is. His cigarette seems to be waiting for her. She takes it, but she's suspicious.*

DOREEN: What are you doin' here?
EARL: Just gimme some coffee will ya, babe?
DOREEN: Are you workin', Earl?
EARL: Yeah.
DOREEN: You got somebody in the car?
EARL: Yeah.
DOREEN: How come you got 'em here?
EARL: They're passed out. It's one of those drive arounds.
DOREEN: You're not drinkin' are you?
EARL: Will you just gimme some coffee?

> DOREEN *pours* EARL *a cup of coffee.*

EARL: I come all the way down here to see you, you think you'd be happy to see me.

> DOREEN *starts to walk away but she gives* EARL *a loving nudge. He smiles as she walks off.*

EXT—L.A. SKYLINE—NIGHT

> *The helicopters fly in formation over the city.*

EXT—THE LOW NOTE—NIGHT

> *The CAMERA TILTS from the helicopters to this jazz club. As the roar of the helicopters subsides, we hear music:* TESS TRAINER *is singing "Prisoner Of Life".*

INT—THE LOW NOTE—NIGHT

> TESS TRAINER *is on stage accompanied by her back-up group.*

> BILL *and* HONEY BUSH *sit at a table with their neighbors,* JIM *and* HARRIET STONE. *The* WAITRESS *serves two more shots.* JIM *hands her a credit card.*

HARRIET: I've cancelled the Times and stopped the mail. All you have to do is check up every now and then and feed the fish.

> BILL *is looking at the audience, mostly black.* JIM *seems preoccupied.*

HONEY: I've got it all written down. *(to* BILL*)* Didn't I put it on the fridge?
BILL: Yeah. She wrote it down. I watched her.
HONEY: So I got it written down. But just come back in the morning.
HARRIET: But you are going to—?
HONEY: Your fish are gonna be fine.

BILL *leans over to* HONEY.

BILL: What about the live fish? Feeding the live fish.
HONEY: Oh, that was a joke, honey.
HARRIET: No, lion fish like goldfish.
BILL: That's what she wrote down.
HARRIET: Yes, you feed them goldfish. Live goldfish.
HONEY: No!
HARRIET: Yes.
BILL: Yeah, we got the goldfish.
HONEY: I thought you were joking.
HARRIET: No.
HONEY: *(to* BILL*)* You do that.

EXT—SKY OVER L.A.—NIGHT

The helicopters continue their night mission.

INT—SHEPARD HOUSE/LIVING ROOM—NIGHT

The dog, SUZY, *starts barking.* SHERRI SHEPARD *is reading a story to* AUSTIN, *the youngest child.* WILL *and* SANDY *are playing by themselves.* HOWARD FINNIGAN'S *editorial continues on the television. Moments later* SHERRI SHEPARD *hears the helicopters approaching. Suddenly there is turmoil.*

SHERRI: Gene, the helicopters are here! Shut the windows!

SHERRI *leaves* AUSTIN *with* SANDY.

SHERRI: Here, watch your brother.

SHERRI *hurries outside to get* SUZY.

SHERRI: Suzy, come here my good little boy.

SHERRI *carries* SUZY *into the house just as* GENE *comes storming into the room.* GENE *takes* SUZY *out of* SHERRI'S *arms. He means business.*

SHERRI: Where are you going?
GENE: The dog stays outside. I told you a hundred times.

GENE *walks outside and puts the dog down.*

SHERRI: Don't put Suzy out this way. They're gonna give her cancer.
GENE: They're not gonna give it cancer. Don't you go gettin' environmental on me, Sherri.
SHERRI: You listened to the news lately? It's dangerous.
GENE: It's not dangerous. They wouldn't be doing it if it was dangerous.

GENE *goes outside and stands with his arms outstretched to expose himself to the spray. A SHOT of the approaching helicopters as they are spraying.*

SHERRI: Oh, yeah! Go ahead. Get cancer!

GENE *storms back into the house.*

SHERRI: What are you doing?

GENE *is after Suzy who managed to sneak back into the house.*

GENE: Get the dog outta here!
SHERRI: Gene! Leave the dog alone!

GENE *chases the dog outside and shuts the door.*

GENE: The dog stays outside. The dog drives me out of my mind.

GENE *storms off.*

SHERRI: Where are you going?
GENE: Out.
SHERRI: This is the third night this week, Gene.

GENE *grabs his coat and is on his way out the door.*

SHERRI: Why don't you start smoking again, Gene?

EXT—L.A. SKYLINE—NIGHT

The helicopters fly in formation over the city.

INT—CONCERT HALL—NIGHT

ZOE *and the* TROUT QUARTET *play* VICTOR HERBERT CONCERTO #2. MARIAN *leans over to speak to the* KANES.

MARIAN: You free this weekend?
STUART: I don't get back 'til Saturday, but if you make it Sunday, I'll bring fresh trout.
CLAIRE: Ha!

STUART *pretends to be reeling in a trout.* RALPH *leans toward* MARIAN *and whispers.*

RALPH: Marian, why did you do that?
MARIAN: What?
RALPH: Invite them to our house for supper.
MARIAN: I didn't. You did.

RALPH: I did?

MARIAN: No, you said let's set a date.

RALPH: I had to say let's set a date because you invited them to our house.

The KANES *are having their own conversation about the* WYMANS.

CLAIRE: He's some kind of doctor. I think he's a dentist. Her name is Marian.

RALPH *is still upset.*

RALPH: Marian, we don't even know them.

MARIAN: Just relax. Okay? Just relax.

INT—KAISER HOUSE—NIGHT

JERRY *and* JOE *are on the floor in front of the television.* HOWARD'S *editorial continues.*

JERRY: Any of those Medflies get on you today?

JERRY *smacks his face like he's swatting a Medfly.*

JERRY: I think I got one.

JERRY *turns towards* LOIS *who is still on the phone.* JOSETTE *is starting to fuss.* LOIS *has her hand cupped over the mouthpiece.*

LOIS: Want me to describe myself for you?

LOIS *spreads a towel on the dining room table.*

LOIS: I'm 36-24-34.

LOIS *picks up* JOSETTE *and puts her on the table to change her diaper.* JERRY *is clearly uneasy with* LOIS' *conversation in the background.*

LOIS: Oh, yeah? Well I'm not gonna suck it.

JERRY: *(to* JOE*)* Come on. Let's go play in your room.

JERRY *takes* JOE *by the hand and leads him through the dining room past* LOIS *changing* JOSETTE. *The baby cries, but* LOIS *goes right on talking.*

LOIS: Can you speak up a little bit, honey, I can barely hear you.

LOIS *keeps the phone balanced on her shoulder so she can use both hands.*

LOIS: Oooh. My panties are getting a little wet.

She uses a diaper wipe.

LOIS: Well, I'm in bed. I'm on my hands and knees. My mouth is so close to your balls.

JERRY *stands in the doorway watching* LOIS.

LOIS: Aah, can you hear that? Can you feel it? Don't you want me to lick your balls first? Mmm, Mmm. Tastes so good. Oh, yeah, baby.

LOIS *picks up* JOSETTE *and tries to keep her pacified while she talks.*

LOIS: It's getting so big in my mouth. So big. Mmm, Mmm.

JERRY *goes into* JOE'S *room and shuts the door hard.*

INT—THE LOW NOTE—NIGHT

TESS *sings "Prisoner Of Life". The* STONES *and* HONEY *and* BILL *are still in the audience.*

BILL: *(to* JIM*)* You don't like the music?
JIM: We got to catch the morning plane.
BILL: Oh well, let's go.

As they leave TESS *finishes.*

TESS: Yeah, I'm a prisoner of life.

INT—FINNIGAN HOUSE/BEDROOM—NIGHT

HOWARD FINNIGAN *and* ANN *are watching the editorial on TV. We hear a child's voice.*

CASEY: Mom?

ANN *scrambles out of bed.*

ANN: Baby?
HOWARD: *(to himself)* Shit.

CASEY, 8, *comes into the room.* ANN *picks him up.*

ANN: Baby? Did you have a bad dream? Come up here, and we'll watch Daddy on TV. We'll snuggle.
HOWARD: What happened, the helicopters scare you?
CASEY: I thought it was an earthquake.

HOWARD'S *editorial ends on this note:*

HOWARD: This is Howard Finnigan with thoughts to make you think.

On the television screen there is a page wipe to the KCAL CHANNEL 9 logo and a caption: Editorial Director Howard Finnigan.

EXT—AIRPORT & L.A. SKYLINE—DAWN

The helicopters are landing.

EXT—AIRPORT TARMAC—MORNING

In one helicopter pilots, WILLIAM "STORMY" WEATHERS, *is unbelting himself.*

STORMY: Go ahead and shut it down. I gotta go make a phone call. It's my wife's birthday.

Other PILOTS *leave their choppers and walk toward the hangar office as a* YOUNG WOMAN *comes out carrying a box.*

YOUNG WOMAN: Okay guys, gather round. It's urine specimen time. It's that time of month, guys, fill it up.

We hear the humorous gabble as pilots take the plastic containers from the box. STORMY *approaches the* YOUNG WOMAN *and takes a container.*

YOUNG WOMAN: Hey, sweetheart, need some help?
STORMY: Cheers!

STORMY *goes to a pay phone. He dials a number and fills the bottle at the same time. (INTERCUT with next scene).*

INT—BETTY WEATHERS HOUSE/KITCHEN—DAY

The phone rings in the kitchen. CHAD WEATHERS, *9, wanders out of his room sleepily to answer the phone. (INTERCUT WITH previous scene.)*

CHAD: Hello.
STORMY: Chad? What're you doin' up so early?
CHAD: It's Mommy's birthday.
STORMY: Hey, that's right. Did Mom ask you to remind me?
CHAD: No.
STORMY: I'll bet she did.
CHAD: *(giggling)* No, she didn't.
STORMY: I'll bet she did. Come on. You can tell Daddy.
CHAD: She did not.

BETTY WEATHERS *walks into the kitchen tying a silk robe. She looks stern as she takes the phone out of* CHAD'S *hand.*

BETTY: Gimme that. You get back to bed, young man. *(into phone)* Stormy.
STORMY: Yeah, how'd you know?

Chad stalls.

BETTY: *(to* CHAD*)* Come on. Two more hours, please.

BETTY *snaps her finger and points to his bedroom.* CHAD *closes the door.*

BETTY: *(into phone)* Who else would call me at the crack of dawn?

STORMY *has filled the specimen bottle. It sits on top of the pay phone as he scrawls his name on it.*

STORMY: Hey, who was that?

BETTY: Whatta you want, Stormy?

STORMY: I just wanted to see what was on the agenda. I got Chad tonight you know. Want to join us?

BETTY *hangs up.* STORMY *holds the phone for a minute then hangs up.*
BETTY *walks back into her bedroom scratching her ass.* CHAD *opens his door and looks down the hall.*

INT—KANE HOUSE—DAY

STUART *comes down the stairs carrying his heavy backpack just as* CLAIRE *comes down the hall. They squeeze by each other as she heads into her dressing room.*

CLAIRE: Oops. Scuse me, sweetie.

While CLAIRE *puts on white makeup,* STUART *fiddles with his backpack closing pockets and loading in his supply of whiskey. We see an array of clown paraphenalia in* CLAIRE'S *dressing room but as yet we do not know* CLAIRE *is a professional clown.*

CLAIRE: I really like the Wymans, don't you?

STUART: Who?

CLAIRE: The doctor and his wife. Marian and Ralph—I think his name is. You know the ones from the concert.

STUART: He seems kinda lofty. You have to work early, huh?

CLAIRE: Yeah, I got two birthdays today. He's a doctor, remember? And she's an artist, I think.

STUART: Oh yeah? What kind?

CLAIRE: What kind? She's a painter. You know she paints pictures.

Outside a car horn beeps.

STUART: There's Vern.

CLAIRE: I think they really want us to come to dinner.

STUART: We'll see. I'm off.

> STUART *stands up and hoists his backpack.*

CLAIRE: What does that mean? We already agreed to go. We made a date.

> STUART *doesn't bother to answer. He's on his way out the door.*

CLAIRE: Bye. Close the door, Stuart.

> STUART *comes back to close the door.*

STUART: Sor-ry.

INT—BETTY WEATHERS HOUSE—DAY

> CHAD *comes out to explore. He looks down the hall in the direction of* BETTY'S *BEDROOM.*

INT—BETTY'S BEDROOM—DAY

> GENE SHEPARD *is in bed asleep.* BETTY *sits on the edge of the bed. As she squeezes a blackhead on the side of* GENE'S *face he jumps.* BETTY *shows him the clock. Suddenly he's in a panic.*

GENE: Oh, Christ . . . Jesus.

> *He climbs out of the bed and starts dressing as fast as he can.*

BETTY: I think it's broken. The little thing didn't come up.
GENE: Why'd you let me sleep? How am I gonna explain this? What is it, broken?

> BETTY *gets her cigarettes.*

BETTY: Yeah.
GENE: Is your kid awake? I don't want him to see me.

> BETTY *lights a cigarette.*

GENE: Is he?
BETTY: Come on, baby, he's asleep.

> BETTY *watches* GENE. *She is calm. He is in a frenzy.*

GENE: Jesus. Kids shouldn't see that kinda thing. Jesus, fucking dog. Fucking dog. Fucking dog knows. I know. Barks at me all the time. How'm I gonna explain this, Jesus. Okay, kids . . . crack kids.
BETTY: What?

> BETTY *offers him the cigarette. His mind is elsewhere.*

BETTY: *(offering the cigarette)* Hey. Arf . . . arf . . .

GENE: What are you doin'? Whatta you gotta smoke for in the morning. I told you I don't wanna do that anymore.

GENE grabs his coat and is off.
CHAD hears GENE's footsteps and ducks into his room. GENE hears the door close, but he keeps on going.

EXT—FINNIGAN HOUSE/POOL—DAY

JERRY KAISER carries his pool cleaning equipment to the back yard. He has to open his log book for the combination to get through the gate.
JERRY hears ZOE next door practicing the Bloch Schelomo on her cello. He looks up and can see her in her room.

INT—BUSH APARTMENT—DAY

BILL BUSH wakes up with a start and finds himself alone. He gets out of bed.

BILL: Honey? Honey? You home? Give me some coffee.

BILL walks into the living room talking to himself.

BILL: Somethin' bit me in the fuckin' head last night.

He sits on the couch, picks up a beer can, blows the ashes off the top of it and takes a swig. He looks around and sees the towel on the back of the couch with the face of a sexy blond woman.

BILL: Hello.

He elbows the face hard.

BILL: Shut up.

BILL hears voices across the way. He goes to the window and lights a cigarette. He watches HARRIET and HONEY on the opposite balcony.

HARRIET: These you can miss. These you can water once a week.

JIM comes out onto the balcony.

JIM: Harriet, we're running behind schedule. I'm gonna bring the bags down to the car.

HARRIET: Okay. All right. *(to HONEY)* So these once a week and these you can miss.

EXT—FINNIGAN HOUSE/POOL—DAY

ANN FINNIGAN *comes out of her house as* JERRY *lets himself in. She is wearing a dressing gown.*

ANN: Jerry, Saturday's Casey's birthday party. The plan was to swim. Howard's nephew's a life guard. We were going to pay him to watch the kids.

JERRY *goes about his work.*

ANN: But I don't know now. Maybe you should drain the pool. Change the water. Won't the Muh, Muth, Muthalanon contaminate the water? They sprayed again last night.

JERRY *continues to work.*

JERRY: It's safe, Mrs. Finnigan. It's only toxic for a few hours. The water actually dilutes it. Water's probably the safest place to be.
ANN: It is so irresponsible. Casey has allergies. The slightest thing sets him off.
JERRY: I wouldn't worry about it, Mrs. Finnigan.
ANN: Why don't you come again Saturday morning. When's your regular next day?
JERRY: Tuesday. I can't make it Saturday.

TESS TRAINER, *the next door neighbor, steps out on her balcony.*

JERRY: But you don't have anything to worry about.
TESS: Hi, Ann. I was wondering if your guy could treat my pool? *(to* JERRY*)* Can you?
JERRY: Can I what?
TESS: Whatever you put in it to kill the bug spray. I'll pay you. I'm afraid to go in.
JERRY: I only have time to take care of my regular customers, Ma'am. I'm sorry.
TESS: Maybe I'll become a regular customer.

CASEY *comes out into the back yard.*

CASEY: Hey, Jerry, can I help with the pool today?
ANN: Casey! Get back into that house. It's still dangerous out here. And you get ready for school.

ANN *hustles* CASEY *back inside.* HOWARD *comes out as* CASEY *goes back in.* HOWARD *is dressing for work.*

HOWARD: Honey, have you seen my wallet?
ANN: Oh, it's next to the telephone.
HOWARD: What's it doing there?
ANN: I was ordering something from this catalogue.

HOWARD: Jesus Christ.

TESS: Will you at least come over and look at it?

JERRY: Not now, Ma'am. I might be able to swing by in a couple of hours.

HOWARD comes back out putting his suit coat on.

HOWARD: I'm late, honey. We'll talk about your bearded Iris tonight.

They kiss and HOWARD rushes off.

HOWARD: Hey, Jerry, how goes the war?

He gives JERRY a pat. JERRY doesn't like it judging by his expression.

JERRY: Bad guys are winning, sir.

TESS finally gets disgusted with Jerry.

TESS: Yeah, well thank you very much.

EXT/INT—24-HOUR CAFE—DAY

DOREEN balances three separate orders. Three men sitting at the counter, STUART KANE, GORDON JOHNSON and VERN MILLER, are talking about fishing.

VERN: Now see these bugs. This Humpy ought to work real well.

DOREEN sets the plates down in front of the fishermen. They straighten out the orders themselves.

DOREEN: Here you are.

VERN: Doreen? Is that your name? Doreen?

DOREEN: That's it.

VERN: Hey, Gordon, wasn't that your first wife's name?

GORDON: Darlene.

VERN: Are you sure?

GORDON: No.

Through the window we see EARL pull up in his white limo. He comes in and sits across the aisle from the fishermen. DOREEN comes over to EARL. She notices stethoscope he is wearing around his neck.

DOREEN: What's that for?

EARL: I thought I might have to examine you later on.

DOREEN: Where did you get it?

EARL: Some doctor left it in my web.

DOREEN: You better turn it in to the lost and found.

EARL: What's the menu like, babe?

JACK LEMMON as PAUL FINNIGAN

BRUCE DAVISON as HOWARD FINNIGAN

ANDIE MacDOWELL as ANN FINNIGAN

TOM WAITS as EARL PIGGOT

LILY TOMLIN as DOREEN PIGGOT

FRANCES McDORMAND as BETTY WEATHERS

PETER GALLAGHER as **STORMY WEATHERS**

LORI SINGER as ZOE TRAINER

DOREEN: The Greek's watchin'. Don't order anything you can't pay for.

EXT—SHEPARD HOUSE—DAY

We see GENE SHEPARD *round the corner fast in the family sedan then immediately turn in the driveway. The kids and* SUZY *run out of the house just as* GENE *is getting out of the car.*

SANDY: Daddy's home! Daddy's home!

SUZY *starts barking.*

GENE: Quiet. Suzy, quiet.
WILL: Bang, bang, bang . . .

SUZY *grabs* GENE'S *trouser leg as he tries to get around the kids.*

GENE: Off me! Shut the dog up!
SANDY: Daddy, are you gonna take us to the park? You promised. You promised.
WILL & AUSTIN: Bang, bang, bang . . . !
GENE: Hey, Suzy. Down, get down. Shut up!
WILL & AUSTIN: Bang, bang, bang . . . !
GENE: Quiet!

The kids are screaming the dog is barking.

GENE: QUIET!

For the moment it's quiet.

GENE: Get in the house.

As SANDY *and* WILL *run into the house* GENE *notices his belt laying on the steps.*

GENE: *(to* AUSTIN*)* You do this?
AUSTIN: The dog did.

INT—SHEPARD HOUSE—DAY

SANDY *rushes in followed by* WILL.

SANDY: Mommy, Daddy's home.
SHERRI: That's really exciting, sweetheart. Now will you sit down and finish your breakfast.
WILL: Mommy, I shot Daddy. I shot Daddy.
SHERRI: Please don't point that gun at me.

GENE *comes in. He's on the offensive.*

GENE: Who gave the dog my belt? This is completely destroyed. It's completely ruined. It's a piece of trash. It's a thirty-five dollar belt!

SUZY *is barking throughout.* GENE *turns and screams at the dog.*

GENE: SHUT UP! This dog has got to go.
SHERRI: You want to talk about where you were last night?
GENE: No, I don't want to talk about where I was last night. Not in front of the kids, I don't. I don't want to talk about the ain-pay and isery-may I saw last night. If you would like to hear about kids on C-R-A-C-K you can come in the other room.

SHERRI *watches* GENE *as he walks out of the room.*

SHERRI: Who's crack are we talking about, Gene?

INT—STONE APARTMENT—DAY

HARRIET *and* HONEY *are standing in front of the fish tank.* HARRIET *is still briefing* HONEY.

HARRIET: I got the list here. All right I've cancelled the Times and stopped the mail. Just come in and check up on the fish——.

JIM *comes through the room.*

JIM: Harriet, Harriet, enough about the fish. Let's go.
HARRIET: Okay, okay.
HONEY: Which one do I feed the goldfish to?
HARRIET: *(gesturing)* These are the lion fish, and these are the gold fish.
JIM: Come on, I don't want to miss that plane. Come on!
HARRIET: Okay.

JIM *rushes out, but* HARRIET *continues her thought with* HONEY.

HARRIET: And you just feed the other fish just regular food.

JIM STONE *carries the luggage by himself down the stairs. He meets* BILL *in the courtyard.* BILL *is wearing a robe.*

BILL: Hey, sorry. You guys are running late, huh?
JIM: Yeah, she keeps runnin' her mouth.
BILL: Uh-huh.

BILL *watches* JIM *struggle with the luggage for a good long time before calling:*

BILL: You need a hand with those?

JIM *turns around but does not respond.*

INT—STONE APARTMENT—DAY

HARRIET *is just leaving.*

HARRIET: Okay? All right? I gotta go. Jim's gonna have a fit. I gotta make sure I have the tickets.
HONEY: Have a good time in Memphis.
HARRIET: Thank you. Now you got the keys.
HONEY: And that's it. Say happy birthday to your mom, okay?

HARRIET *starts for the door.* BILL *is standing just inside the apartment holding a cigarette.*

BILL: Bring back some country ham.
HARRIET: You're not going to smoke in my apartment, are you?
BILL: Oh, no. Sorry. Bye.

BILL *holds the cigarette out the door.* HONEY *walks over to* BILL *and calls down the stairs.*

HONEY: Bye, bye, Harriet.
BILL: They're so full of shit.
HONEY: Oh they been good to us, and you know it. Don't smoke, Bill.
BILL: Brought us to a jazz bar, give us a couple of drinks and what do we do? We're taking care of their apartment free for a month. They're taking advantage of us.
HONEY: Don't you have some classes or something?

HONEY *starts to close the door.*

BILL: I don't punch a time card. I'm not in high school.

BILL *quickly sticks his cigarette inside the apartment and flips an ash before* HONEY *closes the door.*

INT—24-HOUR CAFE—DAY

DOREEN *comes up to* EARL *at the counter.*

DOREEN: So what are you gonna order?
EARL: Ah, let's see, baby. I can't read this.
DOREEN: Honey, put on your real glasses.
EARL: Oh.

EARL *takes off his sunglasses and finds his reading glasses. A quick look at the menu and then:*

36

EARL: Tuna melt.
DOREEN: Tuna melt. It's breakfast. Have a steak and some eggs.
EARL: Not if I have to pay for it, baby.
DOREEN: You're not drinkin' are you? Is that what's startin'?
EARL: No, I'm not.

> DOREEN *has other duties. She opens a drawer where the butter is kept. Bending over her skirt hikes up high giving the fishermen a good view. We hear them react.*

VERN: Whoa.
GORDON: My goodness. My goodness these eggs are good.

> EARL *looks up and around not sure what the excitement is about. As* DOREEN *walks past* EARL *she presses her hand to his. He's still trying to figure out what's going on.*

VERN: Gordon, how about that ass.
GORDON: I've seen better.
STUART: I just saw what she had for breakfast.
VERN: Where've you seen better, *Penthouse*? Come on, I say that's money in the bank.

> EARL *looks on. By now he knows this is about* DOREEN.

VERN: What do you say, Stuart? Seriously.
STUART: Not for breakfast.

> DOREEN *comes back to place an order. She and* EARL *touch hands once again.*

VERN: Scuse me, honey, could we have . . . what was it in bottom drawer you were getting?
DOREEN: What? Butter?
VERN: Yeah, butter. Could we have a little more butter, please?
DOREEN: Sure.

> DOREEN *bends over to get the butter same as before. She gives the fishermen the same view. This time* EARL *sees too.* GORDON *with a big smile happens to notice* EARL *looking on.* EARL, *caught off guard, smiles back like he's one of them.* DOREEN *is oblivious. She looks over at* EARL *which reminds her of his order. Turning to the kitchen:*

DOREEN: Hey, is my tuna melt workin'?

> DOREEN *doesn't see* EARL *get up and leave. As he's walking out he passes* AUBREY BELL, *a door-to-door salesman who figures prominently into the story later.* AUBREY BELL *takes the seat at the counter Earl just left. So when* DOREEN

turns around with the tuna melt it appears to her that EARL *has turned into* AUBREY BELL.

AUBREY BELL: Cup o' coffee.

DOREEN *is flustered.*

DOREEN: Yeah.

She looks outside and sees EARL *driving away.*

STUART: Could we have more butter, please?
DOREEN: *(still distracted)* Oh, yeah, okay. Comin' up.

DOREEN *starts to bend over but suddenly it dawns on her what this is all about. She spins around and catches the fishermen ready to look up her skirt. They know she's onto them. They try to contain their laughter.* DOREEN *faces* STUART.

DOREEN: Is that your face or did you neck just throw up?

They laugh harder.

DOREEN: We're all out of butter.

DOREEN *walks off.*

GORDON: Out of butter . . . Ask for margarine.

INT—WYMAN HOUSE/STUDIO—DAY

MARIAN *is painting and talking on the phone to her sister,* SHERRI SHEPARD. RALPH *walks into her studio eating a bowl of cereal.* MARIAN *ignores him.*

MARIAN: So then what'd he do?
SHERRI: *(on phone)* He walks in at 7: 30 in the morning. The kids are screaming, they're happy to see him you know. Same old story. He sits down. He's acting like nothing happened. No explanation. Nothing.
MARIAN: Are you serious?

RALPH *comes up behind* MARIAN *and looks at the expression on the character in her painting. He mocks the expression.*

SHERRI: *(on phone)* Yeah, I mean nothing. I try to ask where he was and he gave me some—.
RALPH: *(leaning over)* I'm going.
SHERRI: *(on phone)* Where's he going?
MARIAN: He's goin' to work. *(to Ralph)* Okay.
SHERRI: *(on phone)* He gave me some ridiculous excuse like crack kids.

RALPH: *(calling)* Who you talking to?

MARIAN: I'm talking to Sherri. Bye.

> RALPH *walks towards the front door. He picks up his coat on the banister. Meanwhile we hear* SHERRI'S *voice.*

SHERRI: *(on phone)* And then I'm not even supposed to use the word crack in front of them. I don't even want to get into that. Tell me about the Alex Trebek thing.

INT—SHEPARD HOUSE—DAY

> SHERRI *sits at the breakfast table leafing through a supermarket tabloid, cigarette in hand.*

SHERRI: Did he flirt with you?

MARIAN: *(on phone)* Who?

SHERRI: Alex Trebek.

MARIAN: *(on phone)* No. Oh, no.

> *We hear* SUZY *barking and* GENE'S *voice.*

GENE: Shut up!

SHERRI: What's so threatening about that?

> SUZY *starts barking.* SHERRI *turns as* GENE *enters. The CAMERA shows* SUZY *barking at* GENE'S *knee-high boots. As the CAMERA PANS UP we see* GENE *in uniform. He is a motorcycle cop.*

GENE: Sherri, where are my keys?

MARIAN: *(on phone)* Absolutely nothing. But if I so much as look at somebody else, Ralph gets real jealous.

GENE: *(to* SUZY*)* Will you get outta here!

SHERRI: *(responding to Marian)* What an asshole.

> *The children in the play room look up from the television when they hear the commotion.*

GENE: Sherri, you know the dog pissed on the bed again, Sherri.

> SHERRI *just looks at* GENE *as he walks past her to the kitchen.*

GENE: Who are you talkin' to, Sherri?

SHERRI: *(to* MARIAN*)* He's wearing tight pants. He likes it cause it makes his dick look big.

> SUZY *continues to bark.*

GENE: What? I can't hear you. The dog's barkin'.

SHERRI: I'm talking to my sister.

GENE: Yap, yap, yap, yap, yap, yap!

SHERRI: Where are you going, Gene? I thought you were going to have some time off this week.

GENE: I gotta check work. Quality control.

SHERRI: Uh-huh. How about tonight, Gene?

GENE: Sherri . . .

SHERRI: *(to* MARIAN*)* Just a minute.

GENE: You know what kind of work I do, right. Look at me. You know it's dangerous. You know there are things you can't know for your own safety, right?

SHERRI: I was just asking about dinner.

GENE: Don't you worry your pretty little head about it.

> SHERRI *holds* GENE'S *hand. She leans forward to smell his fingers.* GENE *moves off to say goodbye to the children.*

SHERRI: *(to* MARIAN*)* He's outta here.

GENE: All right, kids.

> GENE *walks past* SHERRI *into the kitchen.* SUZY *follows.*

SHERRI: *(to* MARIAN*)* The king is gonna leave.

> GENE *goes out the kitchen door.*

GENE: Come on, Suzy.

> GENE *is out the back door. He coaxes* SUZY *through the doggie door.*

GENE: Come on, Suzy.

> SUZY *goes to* GENE.

SHERRI: Close the gate behind you. I don't want Suzy to get out. He might get run over.

INT—FINNIGAN HOUSE—DAY

> ANN *walks through the house calling up the stairs.*

ANN: Casey!

> CASEY *comes down the stairs dressed for school and wearing a backpack.*

ANN: You are gonna be late for school, young man. Now do you want me to drive you?

CASEY: No, I'll walk.

ANN: Are you sure?

He nods.

ANN: All right, kisses.

They kiss and CASEY *runs out.*

EXT—SHEPARD HOUSE—DAY

GENE *pulls out of the driveway on his motorcycle. We see that he has* SUZY *with him in one of the saddlebags.*

EXT—FINNIGAN NEIGHBORHOOD—DAY

We see CASEY *running to school. He crosses one street to get to the sidewalk. In a SERIES OF SHOTS we see* CASEY *running down a steep hill. We see a car going down the hill. At the bottom of the hill* CASEY *veers into the street without seeing the car. The car screeches and tries to stop but we hear the impact. We see him roll over in the street and lay motionless. The the driver of the car,* DOREEN PIGGOT, *gets out in a panic and rushes to* CASEY. *He begins to move and then sits up.*

DOREEN: Oooh! Honey, honey, are you all right?

CASEY *starts to pick up his books and papers.*

CASEY: I'm fine.
DOREEN: *(picking up for him)* Wait, wait, wait. Let me get your stuff.

He starts to walks to the sidewalk. DOREEN *follows him as* CASEY *starts walking back up the hill.*

DOREEN: Here, wait. Come on, let's get in my car.
CASEY: No, I'm fine. My mom doesn't want me to go in a car with strangers.
DOREEN: No, wait a minute, let me give you a ride home. Make sure you're okay.

CASEY *continues to walk.*

CASEY: I'm fine for sure.
DOREEN: No, no, look. Come on . . . How old are you?
CASEY: I'm eight. My birthday is tomorrow.
DOREEN: I want to see your mom, okay, and dad. See if you're okay.
CASEY: My mom said I can't talk with strangers.

DOREEN *follows, but* CASEY *keeps his head down. He wants to be left alone. Finally* DOREEN *stops and watches* CASEY *trek back up the hill.*

DOREEN: Hey, bye.

41

She lets out a deep sigh of relief. The CAMERA *follows* CASEY *up the hill and lingers on the pedestrian crossing sign he passes.*

INT—BAKERY—DAY

ANN FINNIGAN *looks through a scrapbook of sample birthday cakes.* STORMY WEATHERS *walks up to the counter where the owner,* ANDY BITKOWER, *is working.*

STORMY: Do you have ready-made birthday cakes?
ANDY: Yeah, they're right here.
STORMY: Have you got one with 'Betty' written on it already?
ANDY: Just what you see here. I can do something special, but not for today.
STORMY: Well, all right, I'll take that one. What is it?
ANDY: It's a lemon cake.
STORMY: Can you maybe put her name on it?
ANDY: I can't do it today.
STORMY: Well how much is it?
ANDY: Fourteen seventy-five with tax.

ANDY *takes the cake out of the display case and hands it to* MISS SCHWARTZMEIER.

ANDY: Miss Schwartzmeier could you box it up.
STORMY: Miss Schw . . . Sch . . . Could you maybe just write 'Betty' there?
SCHWARTZMEIER: *Vas?* Betty? No.

ANN *looks up from the scrapbook and sees* CLAIRE KANE'S *Clownmobile drive up and park in front of the bakery.* CLAIRE *gets out of her car in a clown suit wearing clown makeup and a green wig.* ANN *watches for a moment then goes to the counter.*

ANN: I'd like to order a birthday cake.
STORMY: Birthdays. They keep adding up.

ANN *gives him a look with comment.* STORMY *takes his cake and walks to the door. When he sees* CLAIRE *coming he holds the door for her. He has a long look at her before walking out. We hear* ANN *talking to* ANDY.

ANN: I have a couple of ideas here. This is what I'd like.

ANN *takes out a notebook and shows the sketch to* ANDY.

ANDY: Is that supposed to be a baseball bat?
ANN: Yes that's a baseball bat. I don't draw very well.

The CAMERA *follows* CLAIRE.

CLAIRE: Hi, Miss Schwartzmeier, I came to pick up the cake for Debbie Eggen-
weiler. And I think it's prepaid.

SCHWARTZMEIER: Yes.

CLAIRE: I finally got these new fliers. Could I leave them?

SCHWARTZMEIER: Sure, sure.

ANDY: You know I like this.

ANN: He's starting Little League. We're real excited.

ANDY: That's really sweet. His name is Casey and he plays baseball.

ANN: Yeah. Casey. Can you read that? C-A-S-E-Y.

> CLAIRE *gets her cake and walks to the door.*

ANDY: I'll do it like that if that's what you want.

ANN: That's what I want.

EXT—TRAINER HOUSE/DRIVEWAY—DAY

> ZOE TRAINER *is playing basketball with* FIVE TEENAGERS. *She plays vigorous game like she was one of the boys. Dressed in shorts and T-shirt she doesn't seem to be aware of her sexuality. Altogether this is a surprising flip side of the concert cellist seen the night before.*
> CASEY *walks by, head down.* ZOE *stops playing.*

ZOE: Hey, Casey, how come you're not in school?

> CASEY *doesn't answer.*

ZOE: Hey, Casey, want to see that dribble?

> *He continues on as if in deep concentration. The other players are impatient.* ZOE *goes back to her game.* CASEY *crosses the lawn to his house.*

EXT—L.A. STREET—DAY

> GENE *drives by on his motorcycle.* SUZY *is still in the saddlebag. The* CAMERA *stays on the sign as* GENE *passes: ENTERING MEDFLY QUARANTINE AREA.*

EXT—MOUNTAIN COUNTRY—DAY

> *We see the old Jeep Cherokee carrying the three fishermen climbing a steep dirt trail. We can see the three men bouncing around inside as the truck turns from one dirt trail to another and continue to climb higher into the mountains.*

EXT—PIGGOT TRAILER—DAY

DOREEN'S *car pulls into a trailer park. She parallel parks in front of their trailer.*

INT—PIGGOT TRAILER—DAY

EARL *is watching bowling. He's stripped down to his undershirt and he's had a few drinks. When he hears* DOREEN'S *car outside he goes to the window.* DOREEN *slams the door shut.* EARL *takes his glass to the sink and rinses it out. He sniffs to be sure there's no liquor smell. He returns to his chair and starts playing with the stethoscope casually.*
DOREEN *closes the porch door.*

DOREEN: What's the door doin' standin' wide open? Hey, you hungry, honey? What are you doin' anyway? How come you're not workin'? You're not gonna lose your job again are you? You better give that back, some doctor's gonna be lookin' for it.

EARL *continues to fiddle with the stethoscope without bothering to answer* DOREEN.

DOREEN: I got London Broil from the Greek. Want me to fix it? Want me to freeze it?
EARL: Doreen, Doreen, the question queen, stoled a London Broil thick and lean.
DOREEN: How about a fruit plate? Something light.
EARL: How bout a short skirt, Doreen. Short enough so I can see every inch of your ass. How'd that be?
DOREEN: What are you talking crazy for?

DOREEN *walks to the bedroom, unzipping her uniform.*

EARL: Well we don't want to talk about that, do we? We just want to talk about Earl. Let's hear more about Earl. How bout cops, baby, I bet they love those short skirts. I know fishermen like 'em.

DOREEN *gives* EARL *the finger from the other room.*

EXT—MOUNTAIN COUNTRY/FISHING TRIP—DAY

A backpack flies through the air and lands with the sound of breaking glass.

STUART: Whoa, man, wait a second.

The fishermen are unloading the truck. GORDON *and* VERN *look on as* STUART *opens his backpack.*

VERN: What happened?

44

STUART *pulls out part of the broken whiskey bottle.*

STUART: Oh, Christ, that's half my supply.

STUART *flings the broken glass aside. He loads up his backpack and falls in behind* GORDON *and* VERN. *They start hiking in.*

VERN: Okay. All right. Let's go.
GORDON: Watch your step.
STUART: I'm thirsty already.
VERN: Only got three hours and fifty-nine minutes to go.
STUART: Well I don't think it's gonna rain.

INT—FINNIGAN HOUSE—DAY

ANN *comes into the house. She puts her shopping bags on the table, picks up a catalogue and starts to browse as she walks up the stairs. Several steps up she stops and listens. She hears the TV. She comes back downstairs and shuts it off nonchalantly, but when she turns around she gasps.* CASEY *is on the couch, reclining, half asleep.*

ANN: Casey? What are you doing home, honey? Why aren't you at school?

Then she notices that he has a scrape on his forehead.

ANN: Honey, what happened?
CASEY: I got hit by a car.
ANN: What?! What do you mean you got hit by a car?! Where?! How?!

She is very upset seeing scrapes and scratches, but she tries to keep her head.

ANN: Casey, now you tell Mommy exactly what happened.
CASEY: I got hit in the back and knocked down hard.
ANN: Well, how'd you get home?
CASEY: Walked.

ANN *works very hard to keep herself under control. She is helped somewhat by the fact that* CASEY *does not appear to be seriously injured.*

ANN: Casey, let me look at you. What about this car? How fast was it going? Who hit you?
CASEY: She was a lady. She was nice.

INT—PIGGOT TRAILER—DAY

DOREEN *walks in from the bedroom.*

DOREEN: Listen, honey, today something terrible happened. I hit this little kid with my car.

EARL: Oh, God.

DOREEN: Oh he didn't get hurt, I swear to God he was okay, but Jesus it scared the hell out of me.

EARL: Oh, Jesus, all right, were the cops there?

DOREEN: I told you, he wasn't hurt.

EARL: Okay, all right, listen. Did they get your name?

DOREEN: I told you. Nobody was there. He's all right.

EARL: Okay, all right, I just don't want to get sued.

DOREEN: Earl, it was just a stroke of luck that I didn't kill him.

EARL: Well, I'm glad somebody's luck is holding out.

INT—KCAL/CHANNEL 9—DAY

JERRY DUNPHY and HOWARD FINNIGAN are chatting before they go on the air. MELANIE the floor manager interrupts.

MELANIE: Excuse me, Howard, you have a phone call. It's your wife. I think you got time.

HOWARD and DUNPHY exchange knowing looks. HOWARD takes off his microphone and walks over to a phone. We see HOWARD and hear ANN's voice over.

HOWARD: Hello.

ANN: Howard?

HOWARD: Yeah.

ANN: Casey got hit by a car. He's all right though.

HOWARD: Ah, what do you mean hit by a car. What . . . when? Where is he?

ANN: He's here. He's home with me. He's all right. He's not hurt.

The CAMERA turns to CASEY on ANN's bed. He is sleeping.

HOWARD: Annie, Annie, listen to me. Just calm down and start from the beginning. And tell me exactly what happened.

ANN: Well, I put him in bed and he fell fast asleep, but he's all right. I'm sure.

HOWARD: Why did you let him go to sleep? You shouldn't have done that, honey. Jesus Christ, I mean, who hit him? How did it happen?

ANN: I don't know. I came home and he was here. He went to sleep. I should let him sleep, shouldn't I?

HOWARD: No, no, you wake him up and you take him to the emergency room. You gotta get him looked at right away. Call Bob Winslow, no wait. I'll call him. Just hang up the phone. I'll call you right back, okay.

ANN: All right. I understand.

HOWARD: Okay, and don't worry. Everything's gonna be all right. He's gonna be fine.

ANN *hangs up and goes over to* CASEY.

ANN: Casey, we're gonna get up and have some milk now.

ANN *picks up a glass of milk off the bedside table.* CASEY *is unconscious.*

ANN: Casey. Casey. Daddy's comin' home. Casey, wake up.

ANN *puts the glass down and shakes* CASEY. *Then she pulls him close.*

ANN: Casey! Casey wake up!

The CAMERA ZOOMS IN on the glass of milk. We hear the distant sound of sirens.

INT—PIGGOT TRAILER—DAY

CLOSE UP of TV showing a glass of milk knocked over accidentally, spilling on the floor.

ANNOUNCER: Accidents happen every day. Fortunately most are harmless, but some are very serious.

CAMERA pulls back to reveal EARL *watching TV.* DOREEN *is in the kitchen taking some aspirin.*

DOREEN: He's eight years old, I asked him. Tomorrow's his birthday. Such a close call. Everything could have changed. Our whole lives could have changed.

EARL: Yeah, well, I wish something would come along and change our life.

DOREEN: What's that supposed to mean?

EARL: Oh, nothin', but maybe I'm just sick and tired of watchin' you show off your ass at work. You know.

DOREEN: Oh, you're drunk, and you lied to me. Get the hell out of here.

EARL: You want me outta here? You got it.

EARL *is on his feet. He goes to the bedroom.*

DOREEN: You told me you weren't gonna lie no more. That was the deal. No more lies.

EARL: Okay watch me go, baby.

EARL *comes out putting on a shirt and tie.*

EARL: You know a lotta guys don't like a big ass in their face when they're tryin' to eat.

DOREEN: Ah, pick a fight. Go ahead, pick a fight.

EARL: Tell you something, you know I don't know who you think'd want to look at your sad, middle-aged ass anyway.

DOREEN: Don't you talk to me like that and don't you come back. I'm not takin' you back no more. You understand?

EARL: Oh yeah?

DOREEN: No more. No more. I'm not takin' you back.

EARL: I'm not coming back.

EARL is collecting his things working his way to the door.

DOREEN: Slobbering all over Honey like that. It was so embarrassing.

EARL: I didn't touch Honey!

DOREEN: I didn't say you touched her, I said you slobbered on her.

EARL yanks open the flimsy screen door.

EARL: How come you don't wear your wedding ring to work anymore?

DOREEN: Oh you're such a bullshit artist.

EARL storms out.

EARL: You're the one chippin' away at our mansion of love, baby, not me.

DOREEN: Why don't you go get drunk and pee on Irmadine's drapes again?

EARL: I'm gonna get drunk. I'm gonna get drunk right now, goddammit.

EARL pulls out a miniature, guzzles some and throws the empty on the ground.

DOREEN: Look how stupid you're acting.

EARL guns he engine of the limo and pulls out.

DOREEN: What if I'd killed him, then what?

The limousine disappears. DOREEN looks around and sees her neighbor PAT has been watching the whole fight. DOREEN turns around to go back inside.

DOREEN: Oh, Pat, what are you lookin' at? It's nothin' new. Have a nice day.

INT—BETTY'S HOUSE—DAY

CHAD sits on the floor building something elaborate with Tinkertoys and watching "Captain Planet" on TV. He hears a car door slam. Looking out he sees STORMY running to the door. BETTY comes into the room carrying CHAD's overnight bag.

BETTY: Your dad's here. Come on, let's go.

STORMY knocks.

BETTY: All right I'm coming.

BETTY *starts to hurry* CHAD *to the door. She pauses before opening the door.*

BETTY: I don't want you to have any fun and stay up really late, okay? Give me a kiss.

When BETTY *opens the door* STORMY *bursts in with the birthday cake.*

STORMY: You changed the lock. Happy Birthday!

BETTY *is exasperated.* CHAD *starts talking a mile a minute.*

CHAD: Look at this helicopter. Isn't it neat? It squirts water.
STORMY: Hmmmm.

STORMY *isn't listening. He takes the cake out of the box, finds a regular candle and sticks it into the cake. Then he lights it.*

STORMY: Come on. Make a wish and blow. You're not all blown out are you?

BETTY *glares at* STORMY.

CHAD: Hey, how come there's only one candle? Mommy's twenty-nine.
STORMY: Sure she is.
BETTY: Shut up.
CHAD: That's what she told me.
STORMY: I'm tryin' to get Mommy used to one big candle instead of a lot of little ones.
BETTY: Is that a joke?
STORMY: Come on, blow.

BETTY *licks her fingers and pinches out the flame.*

STORMY: Ooow. You got your wish!
CHAD: What'd you wish for?

STORMY *goes over to the grandfather clock, opens it and takes out a key to wind it.*

BETTY: That you two would get the hell out of here.
STORMY: Oh, Betty, you've got to keep this wound.
BETTY: It's your clock, Stormy. You take it and keep it wound. I want you gone by the time I get out of the shower.

BETTY *leaves.* CHAD *gives* STORMY *a look.*

CHAD: Oooof.

EXT—VERN MILLER'S NEIGHBORHOOD—DAY

GENE rides his motorcycle through a picturesque neighborhood. He sees a yard full of kids. He parks his motorcycle and takes SUZY out of the saddlebag.

GENE: Come on Suzy. Come on boy. Now you go on and run away. We don't want you anymore. Run away. We don't want you anymore. Go on.

SUZY doesn't move. GENE pulls out a bone and lets SUZY smell it.

GENE: Mmmm. Good. *(he flings the bone)* Go get it.

SUZY chases after the bone. GENE starts his motorcycle and speeds off. SUZY has the bone in his mouth. He looks abandoned.

INT—HOSITAL/WAITING ROOM—DAY

CASEY is in bed in an intensive care room. He is wearing an oxygen mask. As the CAMERA PULLS BACK we see ANN, HOWARD by his bed. RALPH WYMAN is behind them talking to a woman who is checking monitors, writing notes, and making adjustments in the machinery by CASEY'S bed.

RALPH: Please make sure you do neuro-checks every half hour and diligent suctioning.

RALPH starts to walk out.

RALPH: Mr. Finnigan.

HOWARD follows him out of the room where RALPH wants to confer.

RALPH: He's resting comfortably. That's good. We'll let him sleep. That's the best thing for him right now.

RALPH looks back into the room and sees ANN coming.

RALPH: The Medfly war. I'm not too sure about that Malathion.

RALPH walks over to the nurses' station.

RALPH: Nurse, can you get me some aspirin. It's for me.

HOWARD comes over to RALPH. He needs to hear more about CASEY.

RALPH: He's got a small blood clot, a little brain swelling, but it probably won't require surgery. He's aspirated but we're not too concerned about that.
HOWARD: Aspirated? What's that?
RALPH: He's got some fluid in his lungs. Listen we'll keep a close eye on him. Okay?

RALPH *walks away.*

HOWARD: Okay . . . okay.

The FINNIGANS *follow* RALPH.

HOWARD: *(to* ANN*)* He knows what he's doing. It's gonna be all right.

RALPH *stops again at the other end of the nurses' station for more aspirin.*

RALPH: *(to* NURSE*)* Three more.

RALPH *turns around and the* FINNIGANS *are still there.*

RALPH: His vital signs are good. We're just going to have to wait 'til he wakes up.

BRIAN WILLIS, *the patient in the next room, is wheeled back to his room after surgery.*

ANN: Was there something we could do? Something we should do?

RALPH: You can wait. There's a waiting room down the hall. Smoking out on the porch if you want to smoke. He may be waking up soon. You'll want to be here when he does.

HOWARD: Listen, how long do you think it will be?

RALPH: You never know with these things. Listen I just want you to do whatever makes you feel comfortable.

EXT—TRAINER HOUSE—DAY

TESS *steps out on the front porch with a Veggie Mary in hand.* JERRY *has returned.* ZOE *and friends are still playing basketball.*

TESS: You made it.

JERRY: Yeah.

TESS: I hope you don't have to put too much chlorine in it. It's bad for my voice.

JERRY *walks towards* TESS. *She points the way.*

TESS: The pool's around the back.

JERRY *walks around the basketball game. He stops for* ZOE *who makes a shot, takes a step back and falls into the bushes.* JERRY *tries to catch but can't.*

JERRY: Scuse me.

INT—MAKEUP SCHOOL—DAY

Half of the students are making up other half in horror movie style: flayed skin, blood, eyeballs out of the socket. The instructor is critiquing the students' work. BILL BUSH *is one of the students doing makeup.*

INSTRUCTOR: See how that bruise is intense but not glowing. Okay, so you want to work on that.

The instructor moves on to BILL'S *model.*

INSTRUCTOR: Let's take a look at yours. *(examining)* This is good. I like that. The bruise is really good. I want you to put a little bit of blood in there.
BILL: In the seal?
INSTRUCTOR: Yeah. Blend out that one edge and take the brush out of your mouth, please.
BILL: Sorry.

EXT—TRAINER HOUSE—DAY

TESS *is out by the pool talking to* JERRY.

TESS: Filter? What's the filter got to do with it?
JERRY: Well if your filter ain't workin, and I don't think it is, then there's not much I can do for your pool.
TESS: How dangerous is this Malathion?
JERRY: How long have you had this system?
TESS: Came with the house.
JERRY: Yeah, well, I hate to be the one to tell you this, but I think it's on its last legs.
TESS: Oh, don't tell me.

INT—BETTY'S HOUSE—DAY

STORMY *cuts the birthday cake into slabs for* CHAD *and himself.*

STORMY: So, Ace, what's up tonight?
CHAD: I don't know. What do you want to do?
STORMY: No, I mean with mom. She's going to celebrate her birthday alone or what?
CHAD: With Gene.
STORMY: Jean, huh? Jean. Jean. Who's she?
CHAD: He's a friend of mommy's.

STORMY *chews a big mouthful of cake nodding and thinking.*

EXT—L.A. STREET—DAY

CLAIRE KANE, *driving her Clownmobile, is pulled over by a motorcycle cop. We recognize* GENE SHEPARD. *He approaches the driver warily, hand on his gun.*

52

GENE: Can I see your license and registration, ma'am.

He watches her every move carefully as she opens the glove compartment.

CLAIRE: Did I do something wrong, officer?

GENE: Take off your sunglasses, ma'am.

CLAIRE: You know this clown is detachable. I have a permit, and it's to code. I've been stopped before. There's never been a problem.

GENE: Phone number, ma'am.

CLAIRE: 504-0361.

GENE: I'll let you go with a warning this time, ma'am. You were driving too slow. Just as dangerous as driving too fast. Please refrain from doing so in the future.

CLAIRE: Can I go now?

GENE: No, ma'am. One more question.

CLAIRE: What's that?

GENE leans down to be eye level with CLAIRE.

GENE: How many clowns can you fit in this car?

CLAIRE: I beg your pardon?

GENE: How many clowns can you fit in this car, ma'am?

CLAIRE: Why did you take my phone number?

GENE: Well, you never know when you might need the services of a clown, ma'am.

CLAIRE: Do you have children?

GENE: No, ma'am. I can use some cheering up from time to time myself, ma'am. Being a cop isn't easy. You have a nice day now.

CLAIRE has the look of someone put upon.

INT—BETTY'S HOUSE—DAY

The television is on to "Captain Planet":

VOICE 1: If there's anything I like more than being mean, it's being sneaky.

VOICE 2: It's a trap!

VOICE 1: Of course it's a trap.

The CAMERA turns to BETTY walking from shower to bedroom with only a towel on her head. She hears something and wraps a towel around herself.

BETTY: *(calling)* Gene? Is that you?

No answer.

BETTY: Chad left the TV on.

> BETTY *walks through the kitchen into the living room and snaps the TV off. She is startled by* CHAD *who sits crouched on the floor eating what's left of the birthday cake.*

BETTY: Oh, my God! Chad. What are you doing here? Where's your dad?
CHAD: He had to go somewhere.
BETTY: Whatta you mean somewhere? Without you?
CHAD: He said he had to do something. Something came up.
BETTY: Yeah, I bet it did. I bet something came up. So what'd he say about you?
CHAD: He said we'd have to do it some other time.

> BETTY *reaches out and takes* CHAD'S *face in her hand.*

BETTY: Hey, he's a sonofabitch. He's a son-of-a-bitch..

> *She moves* CHAD'S *head up and down to agree with her. When she takes her hand away,* CHAD *shakes his head no.*

EXT—FISHING TRIP—DAY

> *The CAMERA PANS DOWN along the course of a rushing river to the bank where the three fishermen are setting up camp. They are pitching the tent.*

EXT—TRAINER HOUSE—DAY

> JERRY *is behind a redwood fence checking out the pool's filter. His portable phone rings.*

JERRY: Jerry Kaiser.
BILL: *(on phone)* Hey, buddy it's me.
JERRY: Hey!
BILL: *(whispering)* Listen I'm walkin' around with a fucking serious chubby.

> BILL *is calling from a pay phone at the makeup school. In the foreground we see* BILL'S *model, in horror movie makeup, waiting patiently in a chair.*

BILL: *(whispering)* Listen to what's going on. There's this girl from Santa Monica high school. She's 18. She's got the body to kill for. Beautiful face. And she asks me to do her full body makeup for this—.
JERRY: Why are you whispering?
BILL: *(whispering)* I'm not whispering, I'm throaty. I'm excited.

> ZOE *enters the pool area all sweaty, dribbling the basketball.* JERRY *turns when*

54

he hears the noise. She shoots the ball into the innertube floating in the pool. ZOE *does not see* JERRY.

BILL: *(whispering)* Listen, so I got to do full body makeup on her, right? That like takes an hour. That means I'm like rubbing base up and down the insides of her thighs . . .

INT—MAKEUP SCHOOL—DAY

As the CAMERA PANS off BILL *and around the room of the Makeup School we see nothing but ghoul faces. No young girls, nothing to suggest that the story Bill is describing ever happened.*

BILL: *(whispering)* . . . like right around her *puddy* and I'm just, oh man, I got to rub it up and down on the inside of her elastic and inside her perfect ass. And I am just like losing it, man. And I was like rubbing some on her titties and she looked up and said, 'what's your name?' And I said my name is Bill. And she said, 'Bill, you're giving me a nipple boner.'

JERRY *watches as* ZOE *takes off her T-shirt and stands bare breasted.*

BILL: *(whispering)* I said that's right. And I was about to like drop my brushes. And this fuckin'. . . . Ooh!

ZOE *peels off her shorts and exercise tights so that she's naked.* JERRY *is watching her and listening to* BILL.

BILL: *(whispering)* It was amazing. Whatta you think about that, man? Pretty amazing. Jer? Jerry? Kaiser?

ZOE *jumps in the water. She floats to the surface face down.* TESS *hears the splash and comes out on the balcony and watches* ZOE *float.*

JERRY: *(whispering)* Oh, uh, did you get a good grade?
BILL: Yeah, they gave me an A+.
JERRY: *(whispering)* That's great.
BILL: Why are you whispering?
JERRY: Shhhh. Shhhhh.
BILL: Why? What are you doing?
JERRY: *(whispering)* I told you I'm working.
BILL: You don't sound like you're working. What are you doing? You working for—.
JERRY: *(whispering)* Okay I gotta go. I'll call you back later. Bye.
BILL: *(trailing off)* You want to have a beer?

JERRY *watches to see what will happen.* TESS *looks down on* ZOE *who is still floating face down.*

TESS: I wish you wouldn't do that. You're not foolin' me, you know.

TESS *takes a cube of ice from her drink and flings down at her daughter.* ZOE *looks around and up.* TESS *is satisfied with herself. She goes back inside.* JERRY *turns away. He is not sure what any of this means.*

EXT—FISHING TRIP/RIVER'S EDGE—DAY

Two of the three fishermen are still fixing up the campsite. STUART *already has his fly rod set up and is about to try a cast or two.* GORDON, *the homemaker, is tidying up the area of their camp.* VERN *is unpacking his stuff, he finds a half pint of brandy and takes a swig, then yells to* STUART:

VERN: Hey, Stuart, nothing counts against first, most or biggest unless we're all fishing, man.
STUART: Yeah, I'm just settin' up this new line, all right?
GORDON: What about settin' up the camp first here? Somebody's got to dig the hole.
STUART: I'll do that. Give me a couple of minutes here.

VERN *puts his bottle away and starts walk over the rocks above the river.*

GORDON: Hey, don't piss on any fire wood.
STUART: And don't piss in the river.

GORDON *works to set up a folding table.* STUART *makes his first cast. It's not so good.*

STUART: Shit.

He hears the sound of pissing into the stream.

STUART: What're you pissing in the water for, Vern?

VERN *calls back.*

VERN: I kinda like the way it sounds.

As he stops urinating and the water clears a little we see something unexpected tangled up in the brush at the edge of the water. It's the body of a young woman, naked. VERN *kneels for a closer look. He can't quite believe what he's found.*

VERN: Hey, Stuart, Gordon, come here a second. Hey, what the hell's this? Stuart come here! Gordon get over here!

STUART *reels in his line fast.* GORDON *scrambles over the rocks to where* VERN *is. They both arrive at about the same time.*

VERN: Holy Christ, it's a goddamn dead body. Look at that, Jesus!

GORDON: What do you think it is?

VERN: It's a dead body, isn't it?

STUART: Yeah it's a woman, huh?

GORDON: She's dead isn't she?

VERN: Yeah dead. I'll say she's dead. Look at her.

STUART: I wonder how?

GORDON: We got to pull her out.

VERN: Pull her out? What are you crazy? I don't think we should touch her, should we?

STUART: No, I think we should call somebody. I think we should call the police. I don't think we should do anything until we call somebody.

VERN: Yeah. That's a great idea, Stuart. You got an Orviz portable cellular phone or something?

GORDON: We can't just leave her there, can we?

The CAMERA stays on the body as we hear the fishermen:

VERN: Well, I know what I'm gonna do. I'm gonna have a drink.

STUART: I think Vern's has the right idea.

GORDON: Hey, wait a minute.

INT—HOSPITAL/WAITING ROOM—DAY

ANN *and* HOWARD *sit. In the background we see* KNUTE *and* DORA WILLIS, *parents of patient in the room next to* CASEY. KNUTE *recognizes* HOWARD *as a television personality. He keeps glancing at* HOWARD.

HOWARD: Look why don't you go home and get some rest? I'll call you if there's any change.

ANN: No, you go. I'll stay here. You go. You rest up. You've got things at the station. I'm all right.

HOWARD: I can make some calls. Probably a good time. But I'll take the number of the pay phone here.

ANN: That's a good idea.

HOWARD: Sometimes it takes forever to get through here.

HOWARD *stands.*

ANN: Could you bring me some shoes, flats and a sweater and maybe mail, a magazine or something.

HOWARD *leans down a kisses her.*

HOWARD: It's going to be all right.

> *As* HOWARD *leaves the CAMERA MOVES IN on the the* WILLIS *couple. They are whispering about* HOWARD.

INT—SHEPARD HOUSE—DAY

> *A small television on the counter shows a dog destroying an upolstered chair. As the CAMERA PULLS BACK we see* SHERRI *making peanut butter sandwiches. She is on the phone with* MARIAN.

SHERRI: Marian? Something horrible happened.
MARIAN: *(on phone)* What?!
SHERRI: Oh my God, this has been the worse day of my life.
MARIAN: Oh my God, Sherri, what happened? What is it? Tell me.
SHERRI: Suzy ran away.

INT—WYMAN HOUSE/STUDIO—DAY

> MARIAN *sits in a chair. She reaches for a jar of peanut butter and a spoon on the table in front of her.*

MARIAN: Ah, Jesus, I thought you were going to say something happened to one of the kids or Gene.
SHERRI: *(on phone)* It's Gene's fault. He's the one who let him out.
MARIAN: I'm sure you'll find her.

INT—SHEPARD HOUSE—DAY

SHERRI: Him. I've been driving up and down the streets trying to find him. The kids are goin' nuts.

> *We see* GENE *drive up the driveway and park his motorcycle.* SANDY *flies out of the house.*

SANDY: Daddy! Suzy's gone.
GENE: Oh, honey, he's out running around. Don't you worry.
SANDY: No he's not, Daddy. He's really gone.
GENE: Honey, he'll come home when he's ready. Don't worry.
SANDY: Daddy, we looked and looked.
GENE: Sweetheart, Suzy will be back as soon as he gets hungry.

> SANDY *follows* GENE *into the house. When the other two children see him they start in.*

AUSTIN: I want Suzy back.

WILL: We can't find Suzy.

GENE: Listen to me. All of you. Suzy will come back. Sometime.

> GENE *tries to get through but the kids grab him and hold on. They're all talking at once.*

SANDY: What if he doesn't Daddy?

> GENE *breaks free.*

GENE: Well, if she doesn't we'll get another dog. We'll get a puppy this time. How's that?

SANDY: *(crying)* I don't want a puppy. I want Suzy.

AUSTIN: *(crying)* I want Suzy.

INT—KAISER HOUSE—LATE DAY

> JOE *and* JERRY *are playing cards in front of the TV.*

JERRY: *(shouting)* Don't you call me that. Now you pick up a card. It's your turn.

JOE: What are you—a pimp or something?

JERRY: I'll come over there and smack you. Know that? Now come on.

> LOIS *is on the telephone at the kitchen table. She is on the business end of a sex-call conversation. She is feeding* JOSETTE *while she talks on the phone.*

LOIS: You don't sound like you're doing it. Now stick it way deep in there. Slut.

> JERRY *gets up from the card game to go get another beer. He walks through the dining from where* LOIS *feeds* JOSETTE.

LOIS: Still got three fingers in your ass?

> JERRY *looks at* LOIS *but keeps going.*

LOIS: Slut. I should make you get an egg. You got an egg in that refrigerator?

> JOSETTE *shakes her head.* LOIS *shakes her head back at* JOSETTE *and smiles.*

LOIS: No, you don't got an egg. What about a candle? What about them rubber bands. I don't think you got 'em tight enough. Snap 'em. Good, yeah, baby.

> JERRY *stops in the doorway looking at* LOIS *and listening to her talk.*

LOIS: Okay take them rubber bands off your dick. I'm gonna suck your dick now.

> JOE *comes in the dining room.*

LOIS: I'm gonna introduce your dick to my tonsils.

JERRY *starts towards* JOE.

JERRY: Sit back down! Joe, now! *(to Lois)* How long you gonna stay on that call, Lois?

LOIS *gives* JERRY *the finger.*

JERRY: *(to* JOE*)* Sit down. Look at the cards.
LOIS: Say please, mistress.

JOE *karate kicks* JERRY. JERRY *fends him off.*

JERRY: Sit down.

JOE *sits but he is still wild.*

LOIS: I didn't tell you to come. Don't tell me you're sorry. Tell me how did it feel. Next time I'm gonna make you get a cue tip with some aftershave and I'm gonna make you stick it up that dick of yours. Three thirty Wednesday. Call me, bitch.

LOIS *hangs up. She writes the call down in her log book.*

INT—SHEPARD HOUSE/BEDROOM—DAY

GENE *is changing out of his uniform.* SHERRI *wants to discuss the lost dog.*

SHERRI: They don't want another dog.
GENE: Well, neither do I.
SHERRI: Neither do I.
GENE: Neither do I!
SHERRI: Neither do I!
GENE: *(shouting)* I . . . I . . . I . . . I . . . !

SHERRI *turns away.*

GENE: I don't even see what difference . . . They're not even gonna know who Suzy is in a week.

SHERRI *sits on the bed.*

SHERRI: All right let's take all the kids, put them in the car and drive around and see if anybody's seen him.
GENE: Can't do it. Got plans.
SHERRI: Oh, Gene, come on!

GENE: Sherri, I told you a week and a half ago I got the Leadership Council thing on crack kids . . .

SHERRI *finds a folded note in* GENE'S *uniform. She unfolds the note and reads it.*

GENE: What you should do is you should go out with the kids, put up some signs, offer a reward—not too much—.
SHERRI: Who's Claire the Clown Kane?
GENE: What are you doin' lookin' in my pockets?
SHERRI: What are you doing with her driver's license and telephone number?
GENE: You wanna know? I'll tell you. Claire Kane, a.k.a. "the clown" is a bunko artists wanted in three states. I have her phone number because I'm running a sting operation. Now you know. And now unfortunately I have compromised yours and the childrens' safety. Are you happy now?

GENE *leaves the room.* SHERRI *holds a straight face as long as she can before laughing.*

INT—WYMAN HOUSE/STUDIO—LATE DAY

MARIAN *is on the phone.* RALPH *comes in and eavesdrops on her conversation.*

MARIAN: There is a hard heavy physicality in my new paintings . . .

RALPH *picks up the phone and listens.*

MARIAN: In part because I've executed them on large panels of wood, but I say they're tempered by the ephemeral use of color . . .

MARIAN *happens to turn around and see* RALPH *on the phone. He acts like he'd just picked it up by mistake.*

RALPH: Oh, sorry.
MARIAN: Sorry . . . Ah, tempered by the ephemeral use of color. I mean you could almost say it's beyond natural color . . . Well, I think they're about seeing and the responsibility that comes with it. Okay. Thanks. Thank you very much. Bye, bye.

MARIAN *hangs up the phone and walks up to the bar where* RALPH *is mixing a drink.*

RALPH: Who was that? Sherri?
MARIAN: No, that was David at the gallery.
RALPH: Oh, David at the gallery.
MARIAN: I'm hoping to get a show there.

RALPH: Is this David at the gallery going to be another Mitchell Anderson in our lives?

MARIAN: What's that supposed to mean?

RALPH: That's the sort of thing you two would blather on about isn't it?

MARIAN: What are you talking about?

RALPH: That lousy painter. The one who never sold anything. Mitchell Anderson.

MARIAN: Just because Mitchell never sold anything doesn't mean he was a lousy painter.

RALPH: So you've said.

MARIAN: Well, it's true.

RALPH: You know scientifically speaking, Marian, there's no such thing as beyond natural color.

EXT—FISHING TRIP/CAMPSITE—LATE DAY

A SHOT of the body in the water. The three fishermen are variously working. GORDON is in the tent loading his camera. STUART is making some adjustments on his equipment and VERN is gathering firewood.

STUART: You know, I don't know why we're sittin' around here actin' like it was our fault. We didn't have anything to do with it.

GORDON: Yeah. Suppose we never came up here in the first place. When would she have been found? Maybe never. I mean nothing we can do to help.

VERN carries a load of firewood. He sets it down and starts breaking up pieces.

VERN: You know she musta been murdered. I mean, she's naked and everything.

GORDON: Nothin' we're gonna do about it tonight anyway.

STUART: Suppose it floats away?

VERN: Then it's out of our hands. Hell maybe that's what we oughta do. Kick it loose and let somebody else find it.

STUART: Ahh, I don't know. I think we ought to tie it up so it won't float away. Then we can, you know, deal with it in the morning. Whatta you say to that?

VERN: I say we got about two hours of prime trout time left. That's what we oughtta deal with.

GORDON comes out of the tent with his camera.

GORDON: Hey let's take a vote.

STUART: All right by me.

GORDON: Fish now or deal with the body?

VERN: I say fish now.

STUART: Suppose the current takes it away?

They take a drink.

GORDON: Then it's not our problem.

INT—24-HOUR CAFE—LATE DAY

> DOREEN *carries a coffee pot to one of the tables. She passes* BETTY, CHAD *and* GENE *who have finished dinner.* CHAD *is doing all the talking.* GENE *is bored out of his mind.*

CHAD: The Planeteers are trying to save the planet and the environment. All wonderful characters.

> BETTY *points to an action figure.*

BETTY: Tell Gene where he comes from.
CHAD: Tropical rain forests.
BETTY: *(pointing to another)* This one?
CHAD: This is Ma-Ti. His power is heart. And let's see where's his ring?

> GENE *is chewing on a toothpick. He's not listening to word* CHAD *says.*

BETTY: (to Gene) Stormy did this to me on purpose and I'm gonna kill him.
CHAD: This is Kwame. He has the power of earth. Let's say he points his ring at maybe earth——.
BETTY: Chad, you know what? You know what? I think it was really nice that Gene brought us here tonight and I think we should say thank you. Don't you?
CHAD: Mommy, can I go to the bathroom, please.
BETTY: Yeah.

> CHAD *slides out of the booth.*

CHAD: Wait. Where is it?

> BETTY *looks around and sees* DOREEN.

BETTY: Scuse me, Miss. Where's the restroom?
DOREEN: For him? I'll take him.
BETTY: Thank you.

> As soon as Chad leaves, BETTY *slides around to* GENE. *They kiss passionately. She breaks it off.* GENE *wants more.* BETTY *sees the present on the table.*

BETTY: What's that?

> GENE *hands it to her.*

GENE: Happy Birthday.

BETTY *starts to open the gift.*

BETTY: What is it? An alarm clock?

GENE'S *smile fades. He stops her from opening his gift.*

GENE: My marriage is breaking up.
BETTY: Oh, honey, really?
GENE: Really. I can't think of anything but you. Not work. Not the trial. Just you. I think I'm getting serious.
BETTY: Oh, honey, I want to be with you too.

GENE *and* BETTY *kiss.*

INT—BAKERY—LATE DAY

ANDY BITKOWER *is on the phone. Next to him is Casey's birthday cake. (intercut with next scene.)*

HOWARD: Hello.
ANDY: Mrs. Finnigan, please.

INT—FINNIGAN HOUSE/BEDROOM—LATE DAY

HOWARD *is on the phone. He looks like he just stepped out of the shower.*

HOWARD: Ah, sorry, she's not here right now. Who's this, please.
ANDY: *(on phone)* This is Mr. Bitkower. She placed an order today, and I just wanted to make sure I was clear about what she wanted. Her drawing's a little messed up.
HOWARD: Yeah, well she isn't here right now. Why don't you call back next week. All right?

He hangs up abruptly and heads back to the bathroom. The phone rings again. HOWARD *returns to answer it.*

HOWARD: Hello.
ANDY: *(on phone)* I don't appreciate being hung up on when I'm calling about your order. I need to know whether Mrs. Finnigan wants a bat or a mitt. Now may I speak to her please?
HOWARD: No, you may not, and whatever it is why don't you just cancel it and stop calling all right? Now we got a problem here. We don't need the line tied up with unimportant stuff.

He hangs up and starts back too the bathroom. The phone rings again. He picks it up again:

ANDY: *(on phone)* Look either you give me an answer now—.
HOWARD: Fuck you, asshole! Fuck you!

> HOWARD *slams down the phone and goes back to the bathroom. A moment later the phone rings. The CAMERA moves in on the phone as it continues to ring. Howard's voice from the bathroom:*

HOWARD: Goddammit!

INT—24-HOUR CAFE—LATE DAY

> BETTY *and* GENE *are still in the booth alone.*

GENE: You know it's not easy on me, these hours you know. All right tomorrow night we'll get a motel room.
BETTY: When?
GENE: Tomorrow night.
BETTY: Oh, no, I can't. Goin' away for the weekend.
GENE: What?
BETTY: Goin' to Tahoe to see my sister.
GENE: Tahoe? When did that get decided?
BETTY: I don't know. Last week.
GENE: Your sister? I thought your sister lived in Michigan.
BETTY: That's Phyllis. This is Bunny. Bunny lives in Tahoe.
GENE: Bunny? Who's Bunny? You never mentioned her before.
BETTY: Yes I did. She's my half-sister.
GENE: Half-sister?
BETTY: Gene, you were always with your family on the weekend. How was I supposed to know you could get away?
GENE: Oh, well, I don't know what to think, Betty. Who is this Bunny? Your mother's kid or your father's kid.
BETTY: Bunny? She's really my half-step-sister. My dad's wife's kid. We've been planning to get together for about a year now.
GENE: Oh yeah? What's she do in Tahoe?
BETTY: What?
GENE: What does she do in Tahoe? She married? Tahoe's a fancy place to live, you know.
BETTY: Gene, stop this. I'm going away for a few days to visit my sister. Don't try to make me feel guilty about nothing.

> CHAD *returns to the table.*

BETTY: Making mountains out of mole hills. Come on.

> *She tries to kiss* GENE.

ANNIE ROSS as TESS TRAINER

ANNE ARCHER as CLAIRE KANE

FRED WARD as STUART KANE

MADELEINE STOWE as SHERRI SHEPARD

TIM ROBBINS as **GENE SHEPARD**

JULIANNE MOORE as MARIAN WYMAN

MATTHEW MODINE as RALPH WYMAN

BUCK HENRY as GORDON JOHNSON

GENE: Shhh. Kid's back.

CHAD: There's this really neat camera up front. It's not a real camera———.

BETTY: Find the bathroom okay?

CHAD: Yeah. There's a man throwing up in there.

BETTY: Oh my God. How awful. Is he all right?

GENE: Chad?

CHAD: I don't know. Anyway it's really neat.

GENE: (to CHAD) You goin' to visit Aunt Bunny this weekend?

BETTY: How about those peas. Let's eat up those peas.

CHAD: Bunny?

BETTY: He's too young to remember Bunny.

GENE: He doesn't remember Bunny?

BETTY: Eat 'em up.

CHAD: Anyway it squirts water.

BETTY: Don't bother Gene.

CHAD: It looks like a real camera, please. I really want it. Come on. Daddy would buy it for me.

INT—THE LOW NOTE—NIGHT

EARL *is by himself. He goes to the bar and sits.* JOE ROBBINS *and two other men in suits are standing next to where* EARL *sits.* JAY *the bartender comes up to* EARL.

JAY: What can I get you, pal?

EARL: Same, Jay.

JOE ROBBINS *begins to talk as the band plays.*

JOE ROBBINS: They had not heard the Joe Robbins legend. Are you laughin' at me?

OTHER MAN: No one's laughin' at you. Go ahead.

JOE: I'm on the inside, right? Next to my cell, big Spanish brother. Six-four, six-five. Eddie Valdez. We called him Big Ed. You know I said to him, 'Big Ed, don't fuck with me'. Cat fuck with me. I got my hands on 30 feet of rope. Now you may wonder how I got rope in prison. Like I told you I'm Joe Robbins. Inside or out. You get me? I go in my cell with the rope. Tie up one end.

TESS *is on stage. We manage to hear* JOE ROBBINS' *story throughout the music.*

JOE: Put a noose at the other and I sit back and lay low like a black cat in the shadows. Get me?

TESS: Here's a song I wanna sing for myself.

66

Tess starts singing "Conversation On A Barstool".

JOE: I wait for this big Spanish motherfucker to come moseying down. Soon as he cross my path, BOOM! Like flies on shit, go on this boy, snap that rope noose around his neck so quick and push him over the fuckin' guard rail. The rope snaps tight. His fuckin' head pops off. His body keeps plummeting downwards. And he falls neck hole first into the ground. My point is, Big Ed pissed me off just a little bit. You pissin' me off a whole lot.

Earl leans over to the JOE ROBBINS' group.

EARL: You wanna keep it down so the lady can sing here?

The look that JOE ROBBINS gives EARL tells EARL to back off.

EARL: I made a mistake.
JOE: Hey, you made a mistake.

The two men with JOE ROBBINS laugh.

JOE: Hey, shut up. Shut up I was tellin' a story. Where was I?

INT—HOSPITAL/CASEY'S ROOM—NIGHT

ANN sits by CASEY holding his hand. Behind the bed are monitors—EKG, arterial pressure, pulse oxygenation, and automatic blood pressure. ANN watches a nurse jot down various readings then leave without saying anything.
HOWARD returns after being home. He and KNUTE WILLIS nod to each other in the hall before HOWARD turns into Casey's room.

HOWARD: Hi, how's it going?
ANN: He's still asleep. He really hasn't moved.

HOWARD looks at all the monitors.

HOWARD: What's all this?
ANN: I don't know. Dr. Wyman ordered it.
HOWARD: Any change?
ANN: He says the numbers look good.

HOWARD sits down on the bed.

ANN: I don't think it's a good he keeps sleeping like this. I don't think that's a good sign.
HOWARD: Oh, he's okay. He's gonna be all right. He'll wake up soon. I talked to Bob Winslow. He's in Hawaii. He knows this Wyman fellow. He says we're in good hands. He knows what's what.
ANN: Good. I'm gonna go get a cup of coffee. You stay with Casey.

ANN *stands up and puts on her sweater.*

ANN: Oh, God, why won't he wake up?

INT—THE LOW NOTE—NIGHT

TESS *sings.* EARL *sits at the bar getting drunk.*

EXT—FISHING TRIP/RIVER BANK—NIGHT

The three fishermen using flashlights are tying up the body so it doesn't float away.

STUART: Hey, gimme that. Gimme that. I'll tie it around her wrist.

GORDON *helps with the line.*

GORDON: Never thought I'd be doin' anything like this.
STUART: Yeah, me neither.

STUART *ties the line to her wrist.*

VERN: What's she feel like, Stuart? Feel her tits?

The other two ignore him.

VERN: I just realized. There are probably a thousand guys in L.A. who'd be ballin' her right now.
GORDON: Ah, will you shut up!
VERN: I'm just tryin' to lighten things up a little. All right?
STUART: Let's get the hell outta here. Come on tie that up.
VERN: Man if you'da told me I was foolin' around with a dead body up here I'da told you you were full of shit.

GORDON *ties the line to a rock.*

GORDON: Yeah, okay, let's go.

The fishermen climb back over the rocks. CAMERA PANS DOWN on the body.

EXT—BUSH APARTMENT—DAY

BILL *comes down the stairs and crosses the courtyard heading to the garage. He changes his mind. Instead of going to the garage he climbs the stairs to the* STONE *APARTMENT.*

INT—STONE APARTMENT—DAY

> HONEY *stares at the aquarium. Seen through the glass she appears to be trans-fixed by the fish.* BILL *opens the door and pokes his head in. He can see that* HONEY *is preoccupied. He creeps up behind her.*

BILL: Stop stealing.

HONEY: *(jumping)* God, Bill, what'd you . . . think, Bill. Bill you scared me.

BILL: I'm sorry. Want a make up? You want a little smile on your face?

HONEY: What time are your classes, huh?

BILL: I'm ditching.

> *She laughs.*

BILL: It's true. Now are you snoopin' around? All you're supposed to do is feed the fish.

HONEY: Look at this one. That's a lion fish, honey.

BILL: Oh, really.

> BILL *kisses* HONEY. *She allows it and then:*

HONEY: Come on. You should go to class.

BILL: All right. *(walking away)* These are strange people, Honey.

HONEY: I know it.

> BILL *opens a cabinet below the aquarium.*

BILL: What's in here?

HONEY: Don't snoop. Don't snoop, Bill.

BILL: Why not?

HONEY: You respect their privacy.

> BILL *wanders around the room.*

BILL: Why not snoop around?

> *He takes a video cassette off the TV.*

BILL: With their hot fudge videos out. Their dirty pornography. These people are creepy.

> BILL *takes out a cigarette.*

HONEY: Use an ashtray when you smoke in here. That's a rule. That's a rule.

BILL: Oh, you brought my ashtray.

HONEY: Our ashtray.

BILL: No, on the list it says that's good for the carpet.

HONEY: Oh, Bill.

BILL: How long are these creeps gonna be out of town?
HONEY: A month.
BILL: You know what? I think we should move in here.
HONEY: No.
BILL: Yeah.
HONEY: We can't do that.
BILL: I think it's the only respectful thing to do.
HONEY: Nah, that wouldn't be right.
BILL: Why not?
HONEY: Cause that's not right, Bill. Okay?
BILL: *(smiling)* She's right.

> BILL *picks up his case and starts to leave.*

HONEY: So, I'll see you around 6: 00, okay?
BILL: Yeah, I'll be home.

> BILL *opens the door then stops.*

BILL: But you know we're gonna do the right thing in their bed tonight, right?
HONEY: *(smiling)* Well, ah, I don't know.

> HONEY *is once again absorbed by the activity in the aquarium. The CAMERA follows one of the fish as it glides through the water.*

EXT—FISHING TRIP/RIVER—DAY

> VERN *reels in a fish.*

VERN: Whoo hoo!
STUART: Hey, Vern! Looka here!

> STUART *has a fish.*

VERN: How big?
STUART: It's about three or four pounds.

> GORDON *is also reeling in a fish. He yells to the others:*

GORDON: I got it! Did I tell ya! It's Moby-fuckin'-Dick here. Look at this.

> CAMERA *turns to the body still submerged in the water. We hear* GORDON'S *voice.*

GORDON: Come on baby, come to papa.

INT—TRAINER HOUSE/ZOE'S REHEARSAL ROOM—DAY

ZOE *is practicing her cello (BACH 5th SUITE PRELUDE). She is so absorbed that when* TESS *speaks* ZOE *jumps.*

TESS: How long are you gonna do that? Do you know what time it is?

ZOE *ignores her and resumes.* TESS *sits in a chair across from* ZOE.

TESS: That's Chick's fault. He was always hot for the string players. I always thought they were weird. String players and girl singers.

ZOE: How come—?

TESS: That was his weakness.

ZOE: How come I don't remember him?

TESS: Well, mainly, because he wasn't around that much. Hell, he exploded when you were barely six. Get me another Veggie Mary, will you?

ZOE: Talk more about Daddy.

TESS: Not much more to tell, baby. He was a prick. That's the long and the short of it.

INT—BETTY'S HOUSE—DAY

CHAD *is playing with his pet lizard in the greenhouse window.* STORMY'S *face appears in the window. He knocks.*

STORMY: Wanna get the door?

CHAD: Mommy! Daddy's here.

CHAD *opens the door for* STORMY.

STORMY: Hey!

BETTY *comes to the door. She is furious.*

BETTY: (to Chad) Go to your room and finish what I told you. *(to* STORMY*)* Whatta you want?

STORMY: I came to get my mother's clock.

BETTY: What's wrong with you?

STORMY: Well it is my clock isn't it?

CHAD *is still watching.*

BETTY: *(to* CHAD*)* Finish what I told you.

STORMY *straightens a picture that's askew.*

STORMY: Oh, Betty.

CHAD *closes the door.*

BETTY: What you did to Chad was unforgivable.
STORMY: What, he didn't tell you his daddy's been flying nights? Bombin' the
   dirty Medflies?
BETTY: Get it and get out.

   BETTY *walks away.*

STORMY: Well this house is half mine, you know.
BETTY: Liar.
STORMY: I pay for it.

   STORMY *ambles through the kitchen looking at every detail.*
   BETTY *returns to the bedroom. She covers up an overnight bag on the bed with
   the sheet.*

BETTY: Take whatever you think is yours and get out of my life.

   STORMY *saunters into the room and spots the bulge on the bed.*

STORMY: New sheets. Jungle theme, huh.

   STORMY *pulls the sheet a little exposing the overnight bag.*

STORMY: Goin' somewhere?
BETTY: Yeah, I am.
STORMY: Yeah, where?
BETTY: None of your business.
STORMY: Your condom file drawer is open. You goin' somewhere with Gene? You
   goin' somewhere with Jungle Gene?
BETTY: Get your fucking clock and get outta here.

   STORMY *sees that* BETTY *is getting ready to throw something so he scampers out
   of her bedroom.*

INT—TRAINER HOUSE/KITCHEN—DAY

   ZOE *mixes a Veggie Mary. As she shakes the mixture the glass drops out of sight
   and* ZOE *winces. She draws her hand back, and it's covered with blood. One by
   one she opens her fingers to see that they are still attached.*

TESS: (*screaming from upstairs*) Goddammit, Zoe! What was that?

   ZOE *looks in the direction of her mother's voice.*
   Moments later TESS *comes downstairs and into the kitchen. Blood is every-
   where. She hears a car start up in the garage. She opens the door in time to see*
   ZOE *backing out the driveway.* TESS *slams the door.*

INT—HOSPITAL/WAITING ROOM—DAY

> CLAIRE *the Clown enters with a dozen or so balloons.* PAUL FINNIGAN *is at the reception counter.*

RECEPTIONIST: What was the patient's name?

PAUL: Ah, the boy's name is Finnigan. His father's name is Howard Finnigan, if that helps.

> CLAIRE *stops by* PAUL *to ask the recptionist:*

CLAIRE: Scuse me, I'm Claire the Clown. I'm here to do a party in the pediatrics ward.

> PAUL *smiles as he gives* CLAIRE *the once over.*

NURSE: Yes, I'll call the head nurse.

PAUL: Ah, scuse me, Claire. Do you do tricks in your routine there?

CLAIRE: Uh-huh.

> PAUL *is all smiles as he digs in his pockets and pulls out two shot glasses and an egg.*

PAUL: I got something to show you. I brought this stuff along. I wanted to do this trick for my grandson. He's a patient in there. I used to do this for his dad when he was just a kid.

> PAUL *sets the shot-glasses on the counter one in front of the other. He puts the egg in the glass closest to him.*

PAUL: Now I am going to move that egg from this glass into that glass without touching it. Now you say to me, "How could you possibly do that?"

CLAIRE: *(in clown voice)* How could you possibly do a thing like that?

PAUL: *(mimicking her clown voice)* I'm going to show you.

> *He blows on the egg, and it flips from one glass to the other.* PAUL *gets very excited.*

PAUL: Is that a touch of terrific? It's yours.

CLAIRE: *(walking away)* It's good for bars, but I don't think its exactly a children's trick. *(to* NURSE*)* I'm here.

RECEPTIONIST: The Finnigan boy is in intensive care, sir, but I think that's his mother over there.

> *As* CLAIRE *approaches the the elevator, the door opens and* RALPH WYMAN *and* FERGIE, *another doctor, step out.*

CLAIRE: Dr. Wyman, it's Claire. Claire Kane? You remember. From the concert.

RALPH *just stares at her.*

CLAIRE: This is what I do. I'm doing a children's—. I'm a clown. We're really looking forward to dinner. Stuart's bringing the fish, remember?
RALPH: Right.

CLAIRE *steps into the elevator quickly before the doors close.* RALPH *waves.*

FERGIE: Who is that?
RALPH: I have no idea.

ANN *sits by herself in the waiting room.* PAUL FINNIGAN *approaches her slowly. He's not sure he has the right person.*

PAUL: Ann?

ANN *looks up to see a man she doesn't know.*

PAUL: Ann Finnigan?

ANN *nods.*

PAUL: Ah, great. The girl at the desk said she thought you were—. I didn't want to walk into the boy's room alone, you know.
ANN: Do I know you?
PAUL: Oh, I'm sorry. Paul Finnigan. Howard's dad.
ANN: Howard's dad?

It is obvious that ANN *had never seen Howard's father before.*

PAUL: Yeah, yeah. Howard's dad. I was just passing through L.A. Well actually, I've been living in Riverside for a number of years. Olla filled me in on what was goin' on around here.
ANN: Olla?
PAUL: Yeah, Olla. How's the boy?
ANN: Well he has a head injury—a little clot, and some swelling. But they don't have to operate. We're a little worried because he won't wake up. So, you're Howard's dad?
PAUL: Yeah, yeah.
ANN: Well it was thoughtful of you to come by.
PAUL: Oh, hey, hey, I was gonna come by. But I just heard about this now. You know, I've never even seen him. You know Kevin.
ANN: Casey.
PAUL: Casey, yeah. Yeah, Casey. Howard's doin' real good isn't he?
ANN: We're very worried. You know he won't wake up but other than that he doesn't seem to have any broken bones.
PAUL: No, I mean, Howard's doing real good.

ANN: Oh.
PAUL: The TV editorials.
ANN: Yeah.

EXT—PAY PHONE—DAY

    GENE *has an unlit cigarette in his mouth. He finds the telephone number he wants in his notebook. He calls.*

EXT—BETTY'S HOUSE—DAY

    When the phone rings, STORMY *picks it up.*

GENE: *(on phone)* Who's this?
STORMY: Well who's this?
GENE: Lemme speak to Betty, please.

    BETTY *runs in from the other room.*

BETTY: Gimme that phone!
STORMY: She's not dressed now.

    BETTY *picks up a knife. The counter separates* BETTY *from* STORMY.

BETTY: Give it to me!
STORMY: Honey, put your panties on.

    BETTY *picks up a pieces of fruit and throws them at* STORMY. *He fends them off with the telephone.*

    BETTY *charges around the counter.*

BETTY: Give it to me! Give it to me!

    STORMY *hangs up the phone and hands it to her quickly as he hurries to the door.*

STORMY: Have a nice weekend.
BETTY: Get outta here!

    BETTY *throws another piece of fruit but it hits the door.*

EXT—PAY PHONE—DAY

    GENE *screams into the phone.*

GENE: Hello! Hello!

    He slams the receiver down.

INT—BETTY'S HOUSE—DAY

BETTY *puts the receiver to her ear and as she does she tries to compose herself.*

BETTY: Hello. Betty Weathers.

The line is dead.

EXT—PAY PHONE—DAY

GENE *is upset. He lights the cigarette and takes a deep deep drag on it.*

INT—HOSPITAL/CASEY'S ROOM—DAY

ANN *walks through the doors into the intensive care unit. The* WILLISES *are with* BRIAN. *Two* NURSES *are in the room with a gurney. As they wheel* BRIAN *out of the room,* RALPH *is by his bedside.*

KNUTE: Take it easy. Don't bump him.
RALPH: Let's keep that hallway clear.
ANN: *(to* KNUTE*)* What happened?
KNUTE: They're gonna operate again. It's gonna be okay.

ANN *walks into* CASEY'*s room.*

ANN: You're never gonna believe this, but your father is out there.
HOWARD: My father? Paul?!

ANN *and* HOWARD *walk out of* CASEY'*s room.*

ANN: Who's Olla?
HOWARD: Olla? That's my aunt. Why?
ANN: That's who your father talked to.

HOWARD *sees* KNUTE *and* DORA *leaving the ward.*

HOWARD: What happened to the Willis boy?
ANN: He's in surgery. So when did you talk to him last?

We see PAUL *through the window.*

ANN: He lives in Riverside. That's not that far away.

HOWARD *sees his Father in the window. He veers off, slightly overcome.*

HOWARD: Ahhhh. Well, I don't know. I don't know. This is as much a surprise to me as anybody. I mean I haven't seen him in years. I haven't talked to him since the divorce.

ANN: I wonder why he picked now.

HOWARD *and* ANN *walk out to meet* PAUL.

PAUL *is waiting with outstretched arms, beaming.*

HOWARD: Hi, dad.

HOWARD *shakes his Father's hand.*

PAUL: Hey, son.

PAUL *smiles at* HOWARD *and pats his hand. He couldn't be more pleased.*

PAUL: You are lookin' good. Hey, I'm sorry to hear about what happened to ah . . . ah . . .
ANN: Casey.
PAUL: Yeah, the kid. Yeah but I'm sure he's gonna be fine.
ANN: We're praying.
HOWARD: You met Ann.
PAUL: Oh, sure. I've seen you on television there. You're a real authority. Huh? Huh?
HOWARD: So, ah, it's a bit of a surprise. How'd you find us?
PAUL: Olla.
HOWARD: So, ah, how you been?
PAUL: Oh, pretty good. You know.
ANN: Well, uh, I'm gonna go back with Casey. It was nice to meet you.
PAUL: Yeah, whadn't it.

INT—WYMAN HOUSE/STUDIO—DAY

MARIAN *is painting.* SHERRI *is posing in the nude for her.*

SHERRI: Well, at least he came home last night. That's more than I can say for the dog.
MARIAN: Why don't you say something to him? Tell him what you think.
SHERRI: Oh, he'd just deny it. If I start to get specific about things, he starts screaming about the kind of job he has. He's a pathological liar.

RALPH *comes in the front door.* SHERRI *doesn't flinch.*

SHERRI: To tell you the truth, I'm more worried about the dog.
MARIAN: Uh-huh. I know what you mean.

RALPH *overlooks the studio from the bar area. He is trying to be casual about* SHERRI'S *nudity.*

RALPH: Hi, Sherri. How're the kids?

MARIAN: They've lost their dog. Suzy ran away.

RALPH: That's a shame. She'll probably be back. I wouldn't worry about it.

MARIAN: It's a he. Suzy's a boy.

RALPH: Yeah yeah, that's what I meant.

> RALPH *walks down to* MARIAN.

MARIAN: What are you doing home? You're not supposed to be home now.

RALPH: Well, we have that thing . . . You know the the uh. You know with the uh . . . husband and wife?

MARIAN: Kanes.

SHERRI: Who're the Kanes?

MARIAN: Oh they're these people that we met at the concert. They have tickets next to us. It's not tonight. It's tomorrow night. Remember he was going fishing. We're going to eat his fish.

RALPH: Tomorrow? Oh shit. *(To* SHERRI*)* Excuse me, Sherri.

MARIAN: I told Sherri I'd go home and have dinner with her and the kids. They're really upset.

SHERRI: Ralph, you're welcome to come, but Gene's not going to be there.

MARIAN: I didn't think you'd want to come, honey. You don't want to come, do you? You don't want to come, do you?

RALPH: No, no. I can't. I've gotta work. Some lemons.

> *He turns around and walks off. The sisters look at each other for a moment and then burst out laughing.*

INT—HOSPITAL/WAITING ROOM—DAY

> ANN *and* HOWARD *followed by* PAUL *enter the waiting room.*

ANN: Maybe I will, for a little bit. Maybe, he'll wake up if I'm not here.

HOWARD: When you get home, just sit and rest. Get something to eat. Have a bath. Let's try to, ah, forget about it, okay? Everything's gonna be all right.

> HOWARD *walks* ANN *out.* PAUL *joins the* WILLISES.

PAUL: *(to* KNUTE*)* Scuse me.

> DORA *who's been sleeping sits up.*

PAUL: Oh, sorry, I didn't know you were asleep. I think your son is next to the room of my grandson, you know. Least I assume it's your son. I'm not from around here. I'm just here because the kid got hit by a car.

KNUTE: Are you the father of that news man on Channel 9?

PAUL: Yeah.

KNUTE: I'm Knute. This is my wife, Dora.
PAUL: Oh, she's your wife. . . . Oh, you two are married.

They acknowledge one another.

DORA: I'm sorry to hear about your grandson.
PAUL: Yeah, oh, yeah, he got a cracked skull and a concussion.
KNUTE: Oh, no.
PAUL: But they say he's gonna be all right. He's in shock now.
KNUTE: Well, our Brian, he has been operated on twice. Somebody shot him. On the freeway.
PAUL: What?
KNUTE: Yeah just driving along . . .
DORA: Minding his own business.
KNUTE: And somebody shot him.
PAUL: Oh my God, what's the world coming to?
KNUTE: I don't know. Nobody knows who did it.
PAUL: Jesus. Well ours was like a hit and run too.

EXT—TRAILER PARK—DAY

HONEY, *driving a souped-up Mustang, pulls up behind* DOREEN*'s car.*

INT—PIGGOT TRAILER—DAY

DOREEN *is watching Phil Donahue. She looks out the window when she hears* HONEY*'s car.* DOREEN *has been crying so she takes out a compact to check her appearance. We hear* DONAHUE*'s voice:*

PHIL DONAHUE: He's a recent graduate of Seton Hall University. He drank every day of his college life. Beer and Jack Daniels.
HONEY: *(calling)* Mom?
DOREEN: Yeah, I'm in here.
PHIL DONAHUE: He still loves to get buzzed. He doesn't do it quite as much. But he's not about to give up drinking.

HONEY *opens the door and enters.*

HONEY: Hi.
DOREEN: Shhh. I'm watching.
PHIL DONAHUE: He doesn't think he has a problem. Don't call it a disease . . .
HONEY: What're you watchin'?

DOREEN *points to the TV.*

HONEY: Why do you like that guy?
DOREEN: I love him.

HONEY: I brought you something.

DOREEN: Ah, cute. Goldfish, huh? I haven't seen those in years.

HONEY: I'll set it up for you.

DOREEN: How you feed 'em?

HONEY: I'll show you.

HONEY *puts the goldfish bowl on the TV.*

HONEY: Jesus, Mom, it smells like a bar in here.

DOREEN: Earl's startin' in on another one. I don't know if I can take it anymore. He gets so mean. Didn't used to. We used to have a good time when we drank.

HONEY: How long you gonna to let that guy ruin your life?

DOREEN *lights a cigarette.*

HONEY: Mom! What are you doing smokin' those? You said you quit.

DOREEN: I can't quit smokin' when I got a lotta other stuff going on.

HONEY: Why don't you think about yourself for a change?

DOREEN: I gotta think about Earl.

HONEY: Mom, he's a pig. Do you know that? He's a drunken stupid pig.

DOREEN: I don't want you to talk that way about your father.

HONEY: He's not my father.

DOREEN: Well, he's my husband and don't you forget it.

HONEY *sets up the aquarium.*

HONEY: He's an asshole, I know, Mom. Believe me I know. He's an——.

DOREEN: I don't want to hear that any more. You told that story one time too many. Look at me. He was drunk anyway and you know it. He's all I got. I need company.

HONEY *walks over and sits in Earl's chair. Feeling something uncomfortable she pulls out one of Earl's miniatures.* DOREEN *is too distracted to notice.*

DOREEN: Honey, yesterday I hit a kid.

HONEY: What?

DOREEN: I hit a little 8-year-old kid.

HONEY: No!

DOREEN: He wasn't hurt. I just kinda brushed him, knocked him down. But it was so close. Such a little sweetie too. I tried to give him a lift to his house. He told me his mom and dad told him never to get in the car with anybody less they said it was okay.

HONEY: You were very lucky, you know that?

DOREEN: If I'd been going faster I woulda killed him. Imagine. How could you get over that? You couldn't. I came home. I told Earl our whole life could change. Earl tells me to go on a diet. That's all he could think to say.

EXT—FISHING TRIP/CAMP SITE—LATE DAY

VERN is crouched on a rock by the stream cleaning fish. STUART is cooking. GORDON points his camera at VERN. VERN stands up to pose with his catch.

GORDON: *(to STUART)* Did I tell you? Did I tell you? It's the best fishing I've ever had.
STUART: Yeah. But I lost four of those motherfuckers.

GORDON points his camera at STUART who poses.

GORDON: Yeah but tell me it wasn't worth it. I mean even four hours of walkin' is worth this.

STUART uncaps a whiskey bottle and hands it to GORDON.

STUART: Yeah but what're we gonna do about you know what?

GORDON has a swig of whiskey.

GORDON: I'm gonna take another picture.

GORDON walks off with his camera.

A SHOT of the young woman's body. We hear the camera shutter click.

INT—CONCERT HALL—LATE DAY

ZOE is rehearsing with her group DVOŘÁK CELLO CONCERTO IN B MINOR. Her bow hand is bandaged, but she manages all right. ZOE calls for a break.

ZOE: Bring it down a little bit. Right on the *contabile*. A little bit down I think.
1ST PLAYER: Zoe, is that bothering you?

She looks at her hand.

ZOE: Oh, no. Can we start right at—.
2ND PLAYER: How'd you do that?
ZOE: I fell carrying my mom's lunch tray. Can we start right at—.
1ST PLAYER: By the way, how is your mother? Is she all right?
ZOE: No. I don't think she's got much time left. I can see her change right in front of my eyes. It's a cruel disease. Can we start at number six?

They begin to play.

INT—FINNIGAN HOUSE/DINING ROOM—DAY

ANN *walks in and sets down her bag on the table. She's feeling the strain of this ordeal. She starts across the room when the telephone rings. She hurries to answer it.*

ANN: Hello? Howard?
ANDY BITKOWER: *(on phone)* No, this is not Howard.
ANN: Oh, I'm sorry. Who are you calling?
ANDY: Casey. I want to talk about that little bastard Casey.
ANN: Casey? Who is this!

ANDY *hangs up.*

ANN: Hello! Hello!

INT—BAKERY—DAY

ANDY *hangs up the phone. He picks up a bottle of rum and pours himself a drink. The CAMERA PANS DOWN to the Casey's birthday cake.*

EXT—BETTY'S HOUSE—LATE DAY

STORMY *parks at the corner, across from Betty's house.* GENE SHEPARD, *in uniform, pounds on the front window.* STORMY *nods his head as he watches.* GENE *goes to another window and does the same. No signs of life.* GENE *goes back to his motorcycle, starts it up, and drives off.*
When GENE *is out of sight,* STORMY *starts his car, cruises around the corner and pulls into Betty's driveway. He gets out with him a large duffel bag. He lets himself through the back gate.*

INT—SHEPARD HOUSE/FAMILY ROOM—LATE DAY

MARIAN *is with the three* SHEPARD *CHILDREN who are painting signs for their lost dog. She watches* AUSTIN *and then* WILL *as they paint.*

MARIAN: *(to* WILL*)* This is good. This Suzy?

She walks around to SANDY.

MARIAN: That her tail? That's nice. I like that.

From the living room SHERRI *holds up two beers.*

SHERRI: Marian.

MARIAN *walks up to the table in the dining room where* SHERRI *is sitting.*
SHERRI *slides a beer over to* MARIAN.

SHERRI: Don't let the kids see.
MARIAN: Why?
SHERRI: Cause I don't want to hear Gene's bullshit. He's playing around. I can smell it on him.
MARIAN: Do you think it's serious?
SHERRI: As serious as it ever is.
MARIAN: Why do you put up with it, Sherri?
SHERRI: I just gotta sweat it out. She'll dump him and then he'll come running home to mommy, all lovey-dovey. It's always the same story.
MARIAN: He's such an asshole.
SHERRI: He's just such a liar. Sometimes I ask him stuff just to entertain myself.
MARIAN: Whatta you mean?
SHERRI: To see what kind of cacamamie lie he's gonna come up with. I mean, some of the stories are really fantastic.

INT—BETTY'S HOUSE—LATE DAY

STORMY *lets himself into the house through the back door. He sees the jungle sheets and a silk robe of Betty's on the washing machine.*

STORMY: Betty . . .

He drops them all in the washing machine, opens a bottle of bleach, and empties the entire bottle into the machine. He continues on into the living room where he turns on the TV (KCAL promo). He winds his mother's clock.
He opens the duffle bag, takes out an extension cord, gloves and goggles. He plugs in the extension cord and then puts on the goggles and the gloves. He removes an electric chain saw from the duffle bag, plugs it into the extension cord, takes aim on the couch and saws clear through it.

INT—SHEPARD HOUSE—LATE DAY

SHERRI *and* MARIAN *continue their conversation.*

MARIAN: How's the sex?
SHERRI: Well he's real quick. He's too quick for me. Plus he won't do oral.
MARIAN: Do you?
SHERRI: I used to, before we got married. I would if he'd stop fooling around. I kinda like it. What about you?
MARIAN: Ralph's pretty conservative.

SHERRI: How about other than Ralph?
MARIAN: We've been married a long time, Sherri.
SHERRI: There's never been anybody else since you been married?
MARIAN: No.
SHERRI: Ah, yeah, me neither. Not since the kids.

They laugh.

INT—BETTY'S HOUSE—LATE DAY

STORMY *has his shirt off and is sawing the coffee table.*

INT—HOSPITAL/CAFETERIA—LATE DAY

HOWARD *and* PAUL *sit at a table.* HOWARD *has a bowl of cereal and a banana.* PAUL *has coffee.*

PAUL: This atmosphere sure brings it back to me, son. How many years has it been? Maybe 25 years?
HOWARD: What?
PAUL: Your accident.
HOWARD: Oh, it's about 30.
PAUL: I don't know where all that time went.

PAUL *suddenly remembers the shot glasses and the egg in his pocket. He pulls it all out and puts in on the table.*

PAUL: Hey Howard, you remember?

HOWARD *laughs to please his father.*

PAUL: I brought it to show it to, uh . . .
HOWARD: Casey.
PAUL: Casey, yeah. Speakin' of that, you know, the creek? You can't cross it anymore. They put up a gate, ten, eleven years, yeah, eleven years ago just before I left.
HOWARD: That's good.
PAUL: Course if they'd had a gate that would have changed things wouldn't it? I mean you wouldn't have been in the hospital that day, and hell probably wouldn't be here today. You might not even of had Casey let alone bein' here in the hospital like this. We could still be livin' in Minneso——.
HOWARD: Pop, Pop. Stop it.

84

INT—FINNIGAN HOUSE—NIGHT

A SHOT of the telephone ringing. As the CAMERA PULLS BACK we see ANN *in a chair, not making a move to answer it. The machine picks up:*

CASEY: *(on answer machine)* Hi. This is the Finnigan residence. We can't get to the phone right now, so leave a message after the beep.

BEEP.

BITKOWER: Oh somewhere in this favored land, the sun is shining bright. The band is playing somewhere, and somewhere hearts are light. And somewhere men are laughing, and somewhere children shout. But there is no joy in Mudville, Mighty Casey has struck out.

INT—HOSPITAL/CAFETERIA—NIGHT

HOWARD *returns to the table with some napkins.*

PAUL: You still resent my not being in the hospital with you, don't you?

HOWARD: No I don't. I hardly even remember it.

PAUL: Yeah you do. It wasn't my decision. Things had gotten so out of hand between your mother and me by then, that, hell, I didn't want to be in your room and make it worse.

HOWARD: I don't even remember the hospital. I remember the car flippin' over and gettin' washed away. That's bout it.

PAUL *watches* HOWARD *for a moment.*

PAUL: I did something that day I'd never done before in my whole life. I didn't tell your mother the truth. Called in sick and then I left like I was goin' to work. I didn't tell your mother I was goin' over to Olla's house to hook up a new frige and ice-maker. She'da had a fit. I mean even if she knew I was gettin' paid for my time. She'da had a fit. It was okay for her to help Olla, oh, but not for me, see. She was very possessive that way. Sisters are funny, you know. In this case, I was happy to oblige. I needed the extra money. And it was Olla's idea not to involve your Mother. It was Olla's idea for me to lie. I figured hell it'll take couple of hours then I'll go on to work and tell them I was feelin' better. Anyway I told Olla I'd be over early, and I was, but there was no answer so the door was open and I go in. I hear she's in the shower. I holler out, you know, so she won't get scared when she gets out of the shower and hears me workin' in the basement and so forth. Anyway I go down. After awhile Olla comes down in a robe. And she says she got cleaned up for me. I thought that's very odd to say under the circumstances, but you know Olla. Anyhow she says how's it goin' and I said, 'Fine.' And after awhile, yeah, she asked me if I wanted a beer. She says, 'You want a beer?' And I says, 'Jesus, it's a little early in the morning for that sort of thing, isn't it?' And she says, Well I'm not your employer, am I? Do you want one or not?' I said all right, 'What the hell, why not?.' It seemed like a good idea at the time. She comes back with two beers. I tell you every time I finish a beer, Fwoomp! There's another one in my hand. Christ, now we're up in the kitchen and I'm havin' trouble makin' the joints connect. I'm on my fourth or fifth beer, and I said, 'Olla,' and this is exactly what I said, oh, boy, I will never forget this, I said 'If I have one more beer I'm gonna have to take a nap'. She says 'I was wonderin' what it would take to get you into bed'. Hey I laughed. She says, 'Don't tell me it didn't cross your mind because I'll call you a liar.'

HOWARD *is very uncomfortable. He doesn't want to hear this.*

PAUL: Well I'll tell you the truth, it didn't ever. I found her company attractive, but, Jesus, there was no real—. And, I don't know, I didn't wanna hurt her feelings, you know? I mean, after all, it was your mother's sister. Anyway I don't know how much time passed. All I know is that I am workin' like hell on that icemaker, tryin' to get the damn thing goin'. And she is sayin' things like, 'If the positions were reversed my sister would be doin' the same thing'. Do you believe—? You know like this was some little thing between the two of us. I started sweatin', I tell you my knees are shakin', I don't know what the hell to do. I don't know which way to turn.

PAUL *puts a cigarette in his mouth.*

HOWARD: There's no smokin' in here, Pop.
PAUL: Huh?
HOWARD: No smokin' in here.
PAUL: Oh, that's good. Down to four a day.

PAUL *puts his cigarette away.*

PAUL: And then Wsshht! She opens the robe. And I get a . . . oh, Jesus, God, a look. That woman was put together a hell of a lot better than you'd think when she was just in a dress. I'm tellin' you. Jesus that's hard for any man to resist. I mean, I don't know about you. Sure as hell was for me.
HOWARD: That's a long time ago, Pop.
PAUL: So Fsshht! Neither of us heard your mother come in. Oh, God. She was in such a state. You know she didn't really look at Olla. She looked at me. She said Howard's in the hospital. And on the way to the hospital she said, well, she cried a little bit, but she only said, 'Why didn't you tell me that you weren't goin' to work. They told me you were sick'. Christ, I was so

ashamed. It was an unlucky day. Bad timing. But I'll tell you that first day in the hospital your mother and I stood side by side while those doctors reported to us, and most of the news was bad. But still we stood there together. We took it together. And then Olla lied. God! Olla told your mother we'd been having affairs in the past. It was only that one time. I tried, oh, I tried, to explain to your mother exactly how it happened. You know what your mother said? I don't want you around anymore. I'll get through this alone better. No matter what happens to Howard. I had to respect her wishes, Howard. I mean whether I wanted to or not. I had to. Christ, I kept thinking, you know, some day the truth will come out, and she'll understand. We both know that never happened.

One of the nurses opens the door and comes to the table.

NURSE: Mr. Finnigan, you have a telephone call. It's Mrs. Finnigan.

HOWARD *stands up not knowing where to go.*

NURSE: Oh you can use that phone right there.

HOWARD *goes to the phone.*

HOWARD: Yeah, everything's all right here. You all right?

INT—FINNIGAN HOUSE—NIGHT
ANN: I'm comin' back to the hospital. You want me to bring you anything?
HOWARD: *(on phone)* Why? You should get a good night's sleep. Casey's gonna be all right.
ANN: I'm not stayin' here. That crazy person keeps callin'. I'm scared to death.

INT—HOSPITAL/CAFETERIA—NIGHT
HOWARD: Don't answer the phone, honey. Maybe it's the driver of the car. Maybe she's feelin' guilty or something.

INT—FINNIGAN HOUSE—NIGHT
ANN: It's a man.
HOWARD: *(on phone)* Well, don't worry. I'm here with Casey. The doctors and nurses are with him all the time. He's gonna be all right.
ANN: No, I'm coming.

INT—HOSPITAL/CAFETERIA—NIGHT
HOWARD: I wish you wouldn't, honey.

ANN *hangs up the phone on her end.* HOWARD *walks by* PAUL, *pats him on the shoulder.*

HOWARD: You finish your coffee. I gotta get back.

The CAMERA stays on PAUL, *deep in thought, holding the egg.*

INT—FINNIGAN HOUSE—NIGHT

ANN *is preparing to leave. The phone rings again, but she walks out the door.*

INT—BETTY'S HOUSE—NIGHT

STORMY *smashes everything on the mantle with a sledge hammer, including his own empty beer bottle.*

INT—STONE APARTMENT—NIGHT

CLOSEUP of a colorful painting: two cars of gangsters are shooting at each other. CAMERA PULLS BACK. LOIS *touches the picture.*

LOIS: That is a good painting.
HONEY: Yeah.
LOIS: Really good.

LOIS *walks to another painting.*

LOIS: Colors are good . . . goes with the walls.
HONEY: Yeah but look at these fish though. Aren't they cool?
LOIS: Yeah I don't really give a fuck about fish. They just kinda swim and shit. Hey your makeup looks good.
HONEY: You think it's too much though?
LOIS: No, you look like a model.
HONEY: Thanks.
LOIS: Yeah.

BILL *walks out of the kitchen with a platter of shish-kabob.*

BILL: Almost ready.
LOIS: Billy, you got to do me some time.
BILL: Yeah, sure.
LOIS: Make mine well done.

BILL *walks out to the barbecue on the balcony where* JERRY *is.*

BILL: Hey look at that.

88

JERRY: Looks pretty.

LOIS *and* HONEY *sit at the dining room table.*

HONEY: So what were you saying about virtu—. What is it? Virtu—.
LOIS: Virtual reality. You know what virtual means?
HONEY: Ah, sort of.
LOIS: It's like really real. So virtual reality is practically totally real, but not.

INT—KANE HOUSE—NIGHT

STUART *stands in the kitchen dangling one of the trout in the doorway. When there's no reaction from* CLAIRE, *he steps into the doorway. He sees* CLAIRE *asleep on the couch.*
STUART *shuts off the TV. He holds his fingers under* CLAIRE'S *nose. She makes a face then wakes up.*

CLAIRE: Stuart. I didn't think you were coming 'til tomorrow.
STUART: Ah, you know.
CLAIRE: God, I hate that fish smell. They said on the TV that there was rain up there. Did you get rained out?

STUART *picks up* CLAIRE'S *leg and starts rubbing it.*

STUART: No. Got our limit. And I missed you.
CLAIRE: That'll be the day.

STUART *starts kissing her body. He is starting the lovemaking routine.*

CLAIRE: Your hands stink.
STUART: Kinda smells like pussy, don't you think?
CLAIRE: I hate that.

STUART *raises up, starts kissing her body.*

CLAIRE: Go wash your hands. Stop it.

He opens her legs by spreading her knees apart and pushes his face into her crotch. This is playful.

STUART: Smells like rainbow to me.

She pushes him away but she laughs. She likes this.

CLAIRE: Wash your hands.

STUART *pulls* CLAIRE *to her feet and waltzes her around.*

STUART: Come on, come on, come on.

CLAIRE *is delighted.*

CLAIRE: What are you doing?
STUART: Come on, I been sleeping with men for three days.

EXT—BETTY'S HOUSE—NIGHT

GENE'S *motorcycle comes into view, slowing as he approaches the house. All the lights are on and* STORMY'S *car is in the driveway.*

INT—BETTY'S HOUSE/BEDROOM—NIGHT

STORMY *is cutting up Betty's clothes. He is unaware that anyone is outside.*

EXT—BETTY'S HOUSE—NIGHT

As GENE *crosses the lawn* STORMY'S *silhouette appears in the bedroom window in various poses, but to* GENE *it can only mean one thing.*

GENE: Bunny, my ass!

GENE *picks up a rock and throws it through the window. As* GENE *walks off we can see* STORMY'S *silhouette reacting inside. He's very surprised.*

INT—KANE HOUSE/BEDROOM—NIGHT

CLAIRE *is in bed. She kicks off her panties as* STUART *walks out of the bathroom wrapped in a towel. He drops the towel and gets into bed. They meet each other and embrace.*

CLAIRE: Ummm. Oh yes.
STUART: You have to dry me off.

INT—STONE APARTMENT/BALCONY—NIGHT

BILL *and* JERRY *smoke a joint as they cook.*

BILL: Did I ever tell you what happened the last Pomona game in '83. You remember that game?
JERRY: I broke my ankle.
BILL: Right. Okay well while you were snappin' your ankle, me and Red we slipped mickeys on these four girls. This is true. These like bootleg Qualudes, like dangerous stuff, right? And I remember cause two of these girls names was Kelly. Remember. I think you might have met those two Kellys before.

JERRY *laughs.*
HONEY *and* LOIS *are smoking a joint as they sit at the dining room table.*

HONEY: He doesn't call you, does he?
LOIS: What do you mean?
HONEY: You know. When you're working.
LOIS: Oh, I don't think so. I mean I do get a lot of Bills, but it's a common name.
HONEY: Cause you'd recognize his voice, right?
LOIS: Oh, yeah. Ahhh, it was so weird. The Bishop, my parents' church, called me. Oh, he wanted an incest call like a four-year-old girl. And I look at Joe-Joe or Josette and man, that is fucked up.
HONEY: Oh, man, that could fuck your whole life up. I mean a little 8-year-old girl—she just does whatever the adult tells her what to do. Oh man I know, believe me that's fucked.
LOIS: Hey look I don't condone it, but it's a money call. I mean it keeps 'em off the streets anyway.

LOIS *takes a taste of some dip with her finger and sucks on her finger.*
BILL *and* JERRY *continue their conversation outside.*

JERRY: I like this music.
BILL: Yeah, this is good, huh? It's . . . I don't know, it's different. It's kind of dry. It's like a dry hump, you know. Not some wet pussy.
JERRY: Wet pussy. I know what that's all about.

INT—KANE HOUSE/BEDROOM—NIGHT

CLAIR and STUART *are making love. This is healthy and attractive sex. They finish making love. It has been satisfactory for both of them.*

CLAIRE: You make me very happy.

STUART *is staring at the ceiling.*

STUART: Claire?
CLAIRE: Hmmmm.
STUART: We found a body up there.

CLAIRE *turns to look at* STUART.

STUART: A girl. I guess she was murdered.
CLAIRE: Stuart.

CLAIRE *turns over on her side. At first she thinks he must be kidding.*

STUART: Well when we got there, there she was. Naked body in the water. Just floating there. Dead.

CLAIRE: Jesus. When? Were you fishing?

STUART: No. We just got up there. We were setting up camp and Vern—. *(He laughs)* Vern saw it in the water. I never experienced anything like it before. No one knew what to do.

CLAIRE *is picturing this.*

CLAIRE: What did you do?

STUART: Well, there wasn't much we could do. It was getting dark. And she was dead. Nothing was going to change that.

CLAIRE: How old was she?

STUART: Huh?

CLAIRE: How old was she?

STUART: I don't know. In her twenties maybe. You couldn't tell.

CLAIRE: Must have been horrible. What'd you do?

STUART: Nothing.

CLAIRE: Nothing?

CLAIRE *sits up.*

CLAIRE: After you got her out of the water. Did she drown?

STUART: We don't know. I didn't think we should move her. You know.

CLAIRE: You left her in the water?

STUART: Yeah.

CLAIRE *gets up and walks to the bathroom. This is very disturbing to her.*

CLAIRE: For how long?

STUART: 'Til we left and reported it. I tied her to the bank.

CLAIRE *goes to the bathtub and runs the water. She pulls up her nightgown and sits on the edge of the tub as she washes herself. She is trying to reach some understanding. She stops washing and comes to the door.*

CLAIRE: How long did you leave her in the water?

STUART: Claire, she was dead! We didn't think we should move her. It was dark. We made a decision to leave her there until we could report it. She was already dead.

CLAIRE: And when did you report it?

STUART: This morning. Today.

CLAIRE: Today?

STUART: Yeah.

CLAIRE: And when did you find her?

STUART: I told you!

CLAIRE: Well, when did you catch the fish?

STUART: Christ, that's what we went up there for! To fish.
CLAIRE: You fished while she was in the water. You just left her there?
STUART: Claire . . .

STUART *falls back and stares at the ceiling.* CLAIRE *slams the bathroom door.*

CLAIRE: You're making me sick.

INT—SHEPARD HOUSE/BEDROOM—NIGHT

SHERRI *dressed in her nightgown is pulling off* GENE'S *boots.*

SHERRI: Marian's got a crush on Alex Trebek.
GENE: Alex Trebek? Where'd she meet him?

SHERRI *climbs into bed.*

SHERRI: At a party. He's an art collector or something. She thinks he might buy
one of her paintings.

GENE *laughs to himself.*

GENE: I don't think so. I don't see how she could even give those things away.

GENE *gets down to his shorts and gets into bed.*

SHERRI: She sells a lot more than you think. I posed for her today. Ralph walked
in in the middle of it——.
GENE: Ralph. What a jerk. I don't know if I know a bigger jerk.
SHERRI: It was embarrassing, but they're used to it, being doctors and artists and
all.
GENE: What was embarrassing about it?
SHERRI: Well, you know, I was nude.

GENE *sits up and takes the cigarette from* SHERRI.

GENE: You mean you were naked?
SHERRI: Mm-hm. Nude, they call it.
GENE: You mean like without any underpants?

GENE *eases back down onto the bed.* SHERRI *takes the cigarette from him.*

SHERRI: Wouldn't it be a trip if Alex Trebek bought a nude painting of me?

She thinks about this. GENE *takes the cigarette. We see* SHERRI'S *foot move on*
GENE'S *crotch and start rubbing.*

INT—THE LOW NOTE—NIGHT

TESS *sings "Punishing Kiss." We see* EARL *at the bar drinking by himself.* BILL, JERRY, LOIS *and* HONEY *arrive.* JERI, *the woman at the door, points them to a table.*

JERI: Sit under Art Blakey.

As they walk to their table we see pictures of jazz greats on the wall.

BILL: Where's Art Blakey?

HONEY *spots* EARL *at the bar. He doesn't see her.*

HONEY: *(to* LOIS*)* He's there at the bar. Can you block me?
LOIS: Oh yeah, he's listening to the music. He didn't see you.
HONEY: Can you block me?
LOIS: You're blocked, babe.

HONEY *sits with her back to the bar. The others take seats. We get a glimpse of* JOE ROBBINS *at another table watching as* HONEY, BILL, LOIS *and* JERRY *sit down.*

HONEY: *(to* BILL*)* Earl's here.
BILL: What?
HONEY: Earl's here.
JERRY: *(recognizing* TESS*)* Hey, that's that lady. I just cleaned her pool.

JERRY *has a look around.*

JERRY: *(to* LOIS*)* It's all black people here.

BILL *keeps an eye on* EARL.

HONEY: *(to* BILL*)* Is he lookin' over here?
BILL: Nope. Now he's lookin'. Now he's not.

JERRY *signals* BILL *that he wants to smoke a joint.*

JERRY: We're gonna go.
HONEY: Save me some.

JERRY *and* BILL *leave.* CAMERA *turns to* TESS *on stage.*

TESS: I'd like to sing you some songs that I used to do with my ex, Chick Trainer. That was before he got me pregnant in Miami and before he blew his brains out through the hole in his arm.

During the break in the music, EARL *spots* HONEY.

EARL: Honey, Honey.

HONEY *gets up from the table to meet him.*

HONEY: I don't want to talk to you, Earl. I'm with some people, okay?
EARL: Come have a drink with me.
HONEY: No.
EARL: Come on.
HONEY: Go away you're embarrassing me.
EARL: You're embarrassing me.
HONEY: Go. Go!

EARL *turns around and walks to the rear exit.* HONEY *goes back to the table.*

TESS: Here's a song that says something we've all said at one time or another. "To Hell With Love."

TESS *sings "To Hell With Love."*

LOIS: You okay?
HONEY: Uh-huh.
LOIS: Hey, even if the music sucks here, we're still gonna have fun, right?
HONEY: Yeah.
LOIS: I like this one. The sentiment anyway.

JOE ROBBINS *has been eyeing* LOIS *from the next table. Finally he leans over to her.*

JOE: You lookin' for a friend, Trixie?
LOIS: *(shows off her ring)* I don't need a friend. I got a husband.
JOE: You mean them boys that just left here?
HONEY: Yeah, they're comin' right back, and I hope they don't catch you talkin' to us.
LOIS: They'd probably cut your dick off.
JOE: *(smiling)* I think they went out to get a blow job. That's what I think.
LOIS: And I thought you had to have a brain to think.

JOE *takes two hundred dollar bills out of his wallet and shows them to* LOIS. *This catches her eye. She looks at* JOE.

JOE: Tell you what, Trixie. Why don't you come with me out back and suck on my joint. Hmmm? Hmmm? And I'll give you these two yards. Wanna touch 'em?
HONEY: Would you just leave us alone, please.
LOIS: Honey, Honey, it's okay.

JOE: Come on. Come on. Won't take too long. I just got outta three years of lockup.

LOIS: What's your name?

JOE: My name's Joe, baby.

LOIS: Fuck off, Joe.

JOE *puts the two bills on the table.*

JOE: Oh, Trixie, come on now. You can buy a lot of mouthwash with that.

We see BILL *and* JERRY *as they start to work their way back to the table.* LOIS *moves from the chair she had been sitting in to another chair.*

JOE: Think about it.

JERRY *and* BILL *sit down at the table.* JERRY *sees the money.*

JERRY: *(holding it up)* What's this?

JOE *plucks the money out of* JERRY'S *hand.*

JOE: Hey, I believe that belongs to me, thank you very much.

JERRY *turns to face* JOE.

JERRY: Hey, what's goin' on here?

JOE: You want to say something? *(stares him down)* I didn't think so.

The people at JOE'S *table laugh when* JERRY *backs down.*

LOIS: Hey.

LOIS *just stares at* JERRY. *He feels humiliated.* LOIS *stands up and grabs her purse. She's in a hurry to get away.*

HONEY: You okay?

LOIS: Really coulda used the money. Scuse me I feel kinda sick.

JERRY *stares straight ahead.*

BILL: You got to pick your moments.

JERRY *doesn't answer.*

INT—HOSPITAL/CASEY'S ROOM—NIGHT

HOWARD *is asleep in a chair by* CASEY'S *bed. As the* CAMERA PANS *we see* CASEY *and then* ANN *looking through the window of the room towards the nurses' station. We see a reflection of the nurse in the glass.* ANN *looks worried.*

96

EXT—PIGGOT TRAILER—NIGHT

EARL *bangs on porch door. He's drunk.*

EARL: Doreen! Doreen! It's Earl.

No response. EARL *turns on the lights, fumbles for his keys, opens the sliding glass door and goes inside.*

EARL: Doreen. Doreen baby.

Doreen is not home. EARL *looks out the front window and sees her car. He goes to the trailer next door.*

EARL: Pat! Pat!

Pat doesn't answer. EARL *goes to the trailer on the other side.*

EARL: Wilby! Wilby!

EARL *gives up and sits down, drunk and dejected.*

INT—TRAINER HOUSE/REHEARSAL ROOM—DAWN

TESS *comes up the stairs, looking into* ZOE'S *room.* ZOE *is practicing the cello Stravinski's* BERCEUSE. TESS *comes into the room.* ZOE *continues playing.*

TESS: What are you doing up so early? Did I leave a roach in here? You see a roach? Damn . . . *(she sits on the bed)* I had a lousy night. Couldn't sing for shit. It was a lousy crowd. I hate L.A. All they do is snort coke and talk. *(listens to* ZOE'S *music)* La la la da . . . Yeah, I recognize that. I like that. I wish Chick was here. Maybe I'll get a job in Amsterdam. Chick loved it there. Everyone does. They really know how to treat jazz person over there. How was your night? How'd your hand do?

ZOE *doesn't answer.*

TESS: Chick damn near cut his finger off once. It was in Kansas City. He was workin' with Anita O'Day, and he punched the window of the car out 'cause he'd left his keys inside. It was really a hard time for him to play because the cut was on his slide hand and kept opening up. I knew it hurt him but when I saw that guy walk in the club, I knew it wasn't gonna hurt much longer. He walked straight for Chick. Chick bent down, looked up at me and smiled. Said five minutes . . . five minutes.

ZOE *stops playing and listens.*

LYLE LOVETT as ANDY BITKOWER

LILI TAYLOR as HONEY BUSH

ROBERT DOWNEY, JR. as BILL BUSH

CHRIS PENN as JERRY KAISER

JENNIFER JASON LEIGH as LOIS KAISER

HUEY LEWIS as VERN MILLER

TESS GALLAGHER

ROBERT ALTMAN

TESS: Well I'd heard that before. Five hours later, I got a phone call. Could I please come and get my old man 'cause he had OD'd and they didn't want him in the house. So I got there as fast as I could but he was turning blue . . . *(starts singing drowsily)* Blue . . . and wrapped up in sorrow . . . Blue like there's no . . .

TESS *falls asleep.* ZOE *waits for a moment then walks out of the room.*

EXT—KANE HOUSE—DAY

CLAIRE *comes out of the house to get the newspaper wearing a robe.* STUART *is under the hood of his car. She passes him without speaking. She stands in the middle of the lawn reading the paper.*

STUART: You're up early.
CLAIRE: I have things to do.

She reads as she walks back to the house.

STUART: Work?
CLAIRE: Yes.

STUART *follows* CLAIRE *to the porch. He is being very conciliatory.*

STUART: Aren't we supposed to have dinner with those . . . concert people tonight?
CLAIRE: The Wymans.
STUART: Yeah, them.

CLAIRE *sits down on the railing still reading.*

STUART: Uh, Claire, you know about the other night . . .

She hands him the paper.

CLAIRE: Read the paper.
STUART: Does it say something about it?
CLAIRE: *It* had a name. Caroline Avery. She was 23 years old. She had been raped and then smothered to death. She was from Bakersfield.

She goes back into the house. STUART *reads the paper.*

EXT/INT—24-HOUR CAFE—DAY

EARL *walks in and searches for* DOREEN. *He's a mess. He knocks a stack of newspapers off the cigarette machine but is too distracted to pick them up. He sits at the counter. A waitress ignores him.*

EARL: Can I have a . . . ah . . .

The CUSTOMER *sitting next to* EARL *looks over at him.*

EARL: Some day, huh, buddy?

DOREEN *walks past and sees* EARL. *He is very emotional.*

DOREEN: What are you doing here?

EARL: I'm here to see you. What else? Baby, I looked everywhere for you. I was at the trailer last night. You weren't there. Your car was there, but you weren't there.

DOREEN: Honey, where have you been sleeping? Look at your hair.

She picks some leaves out of his hair.

EARL: I slept outside. I didn't want to sleep in our bed.

DOREEN *is falling for this but is self-conscious about a scene.*

DOREEN: People are lookin'. Wanna order somethin'?

EARL: *(smiling)* Yeah, how 'bout you on a bed of rice?

DOREEN: Cut it out. You want a cup a coffee.

EARL: Oh, yeah, gimme some coffee. How about a egg sandwhich?

DOREEN: With a broke yoke?

EARL: Yeah, with a broke yolk.

DOREEN *pours* EARL *some coffee.*

EARL: Thanks, baby. How'd you get to work?

DOREEN: Peg brought me. I didn't want to use the car after what happened.

EARL: Yeah, right. What time are you gettin' off?

DOREEN: About an hour.

EARL: Whatta you say I chauffeur you around to the manner in which you are soon to become accustomed.

DOREEN: I'm sure.

EARL: I'm gettin' us out of here, baby. I'm gettin' us outta Downey.

EARL *and* DOREEN *touch hands.*

EARL: 'Til the wheels come off.

DOREEN: 'Til the wheels come off.

DOREEN *smiles and leaves.* EARL *watches her. Her skirt is a bit longer than before. He looks around catching the eye of the* CUSTOMER *next to him.*

EARL: Is that a fine lookin' woman or what?

CUSTOMER: I beg your pardon?

EARL: How'd you like to be married to somethin' like that?
CUSTOMER: I am.

INT—SHEPARD HOUSE/BEDROOM—DAY

GENE *and* SHERRI *are making love.*

SANDY: Mommy, Daddy . . .

GENE *and* SHERRI *scramble around trying to separate and cover up as* SANDY *walks in.*

GENE: Silly Daddy sleeping on Mommy.

SHERRI *feigns sleep.*

SANDY: Daddy, Austin's crying and he woke me up.

SHERRI *quickly sits up.*

SHERRI: What is it?
SANDY: He misses Suzy.
GENE: Go tell Austin to come in here and Will too. I got some good news. It's a surprise.
SANDY: About Suzy?!
GENE: Maybe. Now go get 'em and bring 'em in here.

SANDY *leaves the room.*

SANDY: Will, Austin!

SHERRI *dresses quickly.* GENE *slaps his face trying to clear his head. Moments later the kids burst in.* AUSTIN *is crying.*

GENE: It's gonna be all right. Listen kids can you keep a secret? Okay, Daddy did somethin' last night he shouldn't have done. That's why you have to keep a secret. But Daddy went down to the police station and put out an A.P.B. on Suzy.
WILL: A.P.B.?
GENE: Yeah, you're not 'sposed to put A.P.B.s out on dogs, but I did. And I got a call this morning. I think they think they know where Suzy is.
SANDY: Really!
GENE: Yes, yes, and as soon as I have my coffee, I'm gonna go down and see if I can find her. Okay now you guys go ahead and get dressed.
SANDY: I wanna go with you.
GENE: No. Now go get dressed and we'll see if we can't find our little doggie.
SHERRI: Put your clothes on, Will. Do what your dad says.

The kids run out of the room. SHERRI *falls back onto her pillow.* GENE *reaches an arm out across her.*

SHERRI: Gene, not now the kids are . . .

He puts a cigarette in his mouth and lights it.

SHERRI: Oh . . .

INT—BETTY'S HOUSE—DAY

STORMY *sits on the floor cutting up a pillow. There's hardly anything left in tact except his mother's clock. All the furniture has been smashed or sawed up. Even the television cabinet has been sawed on although it still works. Howard Finnigan's editorial, "Tenderness," is playing while* STORMY *works.*

HOWARD: There is a line of prose from the writings of Saint Teresa which seemed more and more appropriate as I thought toward this, so I want to offer a meditation on that sentence.

Saint Teresa, that extraordinary woman who lived 373 years ago said, "Words lead to deeds . . . they prepare the soul, make it ready, and move it to tenderness."

There is clarity and beauty in that thought expressed in just this way. There is also something a little foreign in this sentiment coming to our attention in a time certainly less openly supportive of the important connection between what we say and what we do: "Words lead to deeds . . . they prepare the soul, and make it ready, and move it to tenderness."

The CAMERA PANS across the room. Through the windows we see AUBREY BELL, *a salesman, loading his wares onto a dolly. He is coming to the Weathers' house.*

STORMY *answers the door.* AUBREY *presents him with a business card.*

AUBREY: How are you today, sir? My name is Aubrey Bell. You must be Mr. Weathers. I have something for Mrs. Weathers. She won something. Is Mrs. Weathers home?

STORMY: Oh, she's not at home. What did she win?

AUBREY: I have to show you. May I come in?

STORMY: I'm kinda busy right now. Tell me what it is.

AUBREY: She won a free vacuuming and carpet shampoo. No strings attached. I'll even do your mattress. You'd be surprised what can build up under a mattress over the months, over the years. Same with the pillows.

STORMY: Really?

AUBREY: Yes, sir. This is your lucky day.

STORMY *opens the door.* AUBREY *pulls his dolly up the steps. He is all the way into the house before he sees the destruction. If it phases him, he doesn't show it.*

AUBREY: Well, I can see you've had some kind of problem here, but that doesn't affect my work any. I've seen about everything there is to see.

EXT—L.A. FREEWAY—DAY

We see the Clownmobile among the other freeway traffic. The CAMERA PANS to follow as the Clownmobile passes a sign: BAKERSFIELD 74.

EXT—VERN MILLER'S NEIGHBORHOOD—DAY

GENE's *motorcycle comes over the crest of a hill. He is slowly cruising the neighborhood where he let Suzy go.*
JIMMY *and* WILLIE *are sitting on the front porch playing with* SUZY. GENE *pulls over and parks.*

JIMMY: What do you want to do today?
WILLIE: Go to the beach.
JIMMY: No way. Who's gonna drive us?
WILLIE: I don't know. Look at the cop.
JIMMY: Yeah, cool.
WILLIE: Cops freak me out. He's looking at us.

GENE *comes up the walk towards the boys.*

GENE: Hello boys.
BOYS: Hi.
JIMMY: What's the problem?
GENE: No problem. Have to take that dog, though.
JIMMY: Huh? Take the . . . ?
WILLIE: Why?

JIMMY *runs into the house.* GENE *picks up* SUZY.

JIMMY: Dad, Dad, he's taking my dog.

VERN MILLER *comes out of the house with* JIMMY. GENE *is walking away with* SUZY.

VERN: Hey, hey, scuse me, officer. What's goin' on here anyway?
GENE: How long you had this dog?
VERN: What the hell difference does it make? It's my kid's dog.

GENE: 'Fraid I'm gonna have to take this dog, sir. It's been missing for a couple days. It's highly dangerous. It bit an infant. We have to check it for rabies.

VERN: It doesn't look sick to me. You sure you got the right dog?

GENE: Fits the description, sir.

Some of the neighborhood boys come over to watch.

JIMMY: Please, sir. Don't take my dog. Dad?

GENE: I'm sorry, son, I have to. It's for your own safety.

GENE *walks back to his motorcycle with* SUZY *in his arms.*

GENE: And kids, in the future if you find a lost dog, report it. Every animal has their rightful owner.

GENE *puts* SUZY *in one of the saddlebags.*

JIMMY: Don't let him take my dog.

VERN: *(to* JIMMY*)* Don't worry about it. *(to* GENE*)* Don't you have anything better to do than to take dogs away from kids?

GENE: Keep up with that lip, sir, and I'm gonna have to cite you for an open container.

JIMMY: Aren't you gonna do something? Aren't you gonna get him back?

VERN: Come on, we'll get a new dog.

JIMMY: I don't want a new dog. Frisbee was special.

VERN: Don't worry about it.

INT—BETTY'S HOUSE—DAY

AUBREY BELL *shampoos the carpet.* STORMY *cuts up Betty's lingerie. Neither pays any attention to the other.*

EXT—BAKERSFIELD FUNERAL PARLOR—DAY

The CAMERA PANS DOWN from the funeral parlor sign to CLAIRE *getting out of her Clownmobile and walking to the entrance.*

INT—HOSPITAL I.C.U./CASEY'S ROOM—DAY

RALPH *and* HOWARD, *followed by* PAUL *walk toward* CASEY'*s room.*

RALPH: I asked one of my colleagues to come by, Mr. Finnigan. We're not quite sure why he's not responsive.

PAUL *stops at the nurses' station.*

RALPH: His CAT scan shows the blood clot is still small, but there's still more brain swelling.

RALPH and HOWARD walk into CASEY's room where ANN is.

RALPH: I'd like to suggest some minor surgery. An intracranial pressure monitor.
ANN: Oh, God.
RALPH: Now there's no cause for alarm. Casey's making small improvements in other areas. His lungs have cleared up substantially. That's a big plus.

The CAMERA turns to PAUL at the nurses' station.

PAUL: Brian, the Negro boy in 111. I think he was operated on yesterday. Could I inquire about his condition?
NURSE: Oh, yeah, he's doing well. He's out of critical condition. We'll be taking him out of the ICU today.

The CAMERA turns back to RALPH talking to ANN and HOWARD. They are interrupted by the intercom paging RALPH. He goes to the phone in the hall picks it up and listens.

The CAMERA turns to HOWARD talking to a nurse in the hall.

HOWARD: What is a diuretic?
NURSE: It makes him urinate.
HOWARD: It alleviates pressure?
NURSE: It decreases the fluids in the body.

CAMERA turns to ANN speaking softly to CASEY.

ANN: Casey, please wake up.

CAMERA turns to RALPH on the phone.

RALPH: Okay, I'll be right there.

When RALPH hangs up, KNUTE WILLIS wants a moment with him.

KNUTE: Dr. Wyman I wanted to thank you for saving my son's life. You are a miracle worker.

RALPH smiles but he is in a hurry. He takes a few steps over to the nurse talking to HOWARD.

RALPH: Are you all clear about this?

CAMERA turns to PAUL and KNUTE shaking hands.

PAUL: Hey Knute! Just listening to the good news here. I can't tell you how pleased I am.

KNUTE: Thank you. Thank you. Everybody's been so nice. Things are going great.

CAMERA turns to ANN *whispering to* CASEY.

ANN: Casey, Casey, we love you honey. Please wake up.

CAMERA turns to PAUL *at the nurses' station.*

PAUL: Any change in my Grandson that you know of or . . .
NURSE: I'm sorry, I don't have any additional information.

CAMERA turns to ANN *talking to* CASEY.

ANN: Casey. Casey.

CASEY'S *eyes open and blink.*

ANN: Hey, sweetie. Hey, sweetie. Casey.

CASEY *seems to be trying to force his eyes open.*

ANN: Howard! Howard!

CAMERA turns to HOWARD *in the hall talking to* DORA *and* KNUTE. *He rushes into the room when he hears* ANN *call.*

ANN: Casey's wakin' up. Look, look his eyes are open.
HOWARD: Oh! Hey, Case.
ANN: Casey.
HOWARD: Hey, Case. Hey, buddy, how you doin'? Can you hear me?

CASEY'S *eyes flutter then stop.*

ANN: Casey?
HOWARD: Case . . . Can you hear?

An alarm on the monitor goes off as his pulse stops. The lines on the monitor go flat.

ANN: Howard, what's that? Howard, what's happenin'?!
HOWARD: Nurse! Nurse! Come here!

The nurse rushes in.

ANN: Do something!

The nurse goes to CASEY'S *bedside.*

NURSE: Casey? Casey? Call a Code Blue and get me some help.

We hear the Code Blue call.

NURSE: Code Blue, ICU!

Seconds later doctors and nurses converge on the room. RALPH *is not one of them.* ANN *and* HOWARD *are moved out in the hall.*

PAUL *steps back against the wall and watches helplessly.*

We see the medical team trying to revive CASEY. *They continue to working, but it is obvious that he is dead.*

PAUL *watches. Then he puts his hat on and walks down the long hall.*

INT—FUNERAL PARLOR—DAY

CLAIRE *stands in the back. A* WOMAN *approaches* CLAIRE:

WOMAN: I can't believe it, can you?

CLAIRE *doesn't speak.*

WOMAN: She stayed over at my apartment just two weeks ago. Did you know her from work?

CLAIRE *sort of nods.*

WOMAN: Did you sign the book?
CLAIRE: Not yet.

We see CLAIRE'S *hand with a pen making her signature. When she puts the pen back, however, we see that she actually wrote nothing on the line.*

EXT—FINNIGAN HOUSE—LATE DAY

The FINNIGANS *pull into the driveway.* HOWARD *gets out and walks around to open* ANN'S *door.*

ZOE *and friends are playing basketball.* ZOE *sees the* FINNIGANS *returning home. She runs next door as* ANN *and* HOWARD *walk to the house.*

ZOE: Mrs. Finnigan, how's Casey?

ANN *stops for a moment without responding. She walks across the lawn to* ZOE *and puts her arms around* ZOE. ZOE *is still holding the basketball under one arm.*

HOWARD: Casey didn't make it, Zoe. *(to* ANN*)* Come on, honey. Let's go inside.

ZOE *is obviously numbed by this. And then she turns and runs back into her house.*

INT—KANE HOUSE—LATE DAY

>STUART *is on the phone in the dining room when* CLAIRE *comes in. He watches her as he talks.*

STUART: Well I filled out an application about two weeks ago . . . Mr. Walsh told me to call in case I hadn't heard from him. I've been away . . . family business. Okay, I'll hold. *(to* CLAIRE*)* Where you been all day?

>CLAIRE *is in no mood for questions.*

CLAIRE: What time is it?
STUART: I asked you where you been.

>*The person* STUART *was talking to comes back on the line and he changes his tone.*

STUART: 504-0361, but it should be on the application. Okay, thank you.

>CLAIRE *picks up the bottle of whiskey in front of* STUART. *She pours herself a glass and drinks it.*

STUART: Ah, so this is what it is, huh? Ah, yeah.

>STUART *dials the phone.*

CLAIRE: We have to be there at seven, you know. You don't have very much time.
STUART: What's the big deal? It's just a barbecue. *(into phone)* This is Stuart Kane with a K.
CLAIRE: You made the date, Stuart. Aren't you the big sportsman who's supposed to be bringing the fish?

INT—WYMAN HOUSE/STUDIO—LATE DAY

>RALPH *is in the studio sitting in a chair with a drink.* MARIAN *is straightening up. He looks at Marian's painting of Sherri.*

RALPH: Why are they always naked? Why does naked make it art?
MARIAN: Did you make me a drink?
RALPH: It's in the blender.

>*She goes to the bar.*

MARIAN: Smells strong. I'm gonna have some wine.
RALPH: Is that what you're wearing?
MARIAN: Yes.
RALPH: I thought we were cooking out.
MARIAN: Stuart's bringing fish, remember?

RALPH: If it's a barbecue, why're you getting so dressed up?

MARIAN: This isn't dressed up.

RALPH: I'm not changing.

MARIAN: She'll probably dress up.

RALPH: Are you competing?

MARIAN: Competing with who?

RALPH: Claire, honey. We're talking about Claire. Are you competing with Claire?

MARIAN: For what?

RALPH: What women always compete for, I guess.

MARIAN *shrugs it off. She has other things to do.*

RALPH: Do you think he's attractive?

MARIAN: Who?

RALPH: The husband.

She's noncommittal. She doesn't want to pursue this.

MARIAN: Stuart, it is.

RALPH: He's the kind of guy that women find attractive, isn't he? The outdoorsman type.

MARIAN: We don't know a lot about them. I hope they like something other than chamber music.

RALPH: Isn't it wonderful, Marian, how we can skate around an issue. Always playing our little game.

MARIAN: That's a good idea, a game. It might help break the ice. Jeopardy maybe.

RALPH: I'm talking about us. I'm talking about now.

MARIAN: What about us?

RALPH: You know.

MARIAN: Know what?

RALPH: Let's forget it.

MARIAN: Forget what? What are you talking about?

RALPH: Nothing. It's ancient history.

MARIAN: No, something's on your mind.

RALPH: That party.

MARIAN: What party?

RALPH: You know, what party I'm talking about, Marian. The one with Mitchell Anderson.

MARIAN: Jesus, Ralph. That was three years ago.

RALPH: You kissed him, didn't you?

MARIAN: No.

RALPH: Your lipstick was smeared when you came back.

MARIAN: How would you know? You were drunk.

MARIAN *spills the wine all over her skirt. She grabs a cloth, but she's soaked.*

MARIAN: Goddammit! Look at this! Jesus Christ! Look at this. Look what you made me do.

She hurries off too the kitchen. RALPH *watches.*

MARIAN: Goddammit, I wanted to wear this. Shit.

RALPH: That's the way you looked that night with Mitchell Anderson when you were out necking.

MARIAN *removes her skirt and rinses it under the faucet. She has no panties on.*

RALPH: He did kiss you, didn't he?

MARIAN: Oh, come on, Ralph. I thought we were through with that.

RALPH: I want you to tell me about that night with Mitchell Anderson.

MARIAN: There's nothing to tell.

RALPH: All right then tell me about nothingness. I'd like to hear a complete account of nothing. What you didn't do for two and a half hours.

MARIAN: Why, Ralph? What's so important? It was three years ago.

MARIAN *lays out the skirt on a table as if to dry.*

RALPH: All right it's not important. It's water under the bridge. But what irritates me, Marian, if that's the right word for it, is that you won't tell me the truth. You can't say the obvious. You can't admit that you lied. That's what I don't like— having to play this charade.

MARIAN *comes down the steps in front of* RALPH *to her studio.*

MARIAN: God, Ralph, how did this start? Do you know how this started? Because I really . . . I really don't know how this started.

She gets a hair dryer from her art supplies.

RALPH: Marian! Look at me, Marian! You don't have any panties on. What do you think you are? One of your goddamn paintings?

MARIAN *finds the hair dryer, crosses in front of* RALPH, *and goes back up the stairs. She finds a plug.*

RALPH: I'm giving you the chance to come clean. Clear the slate. On to a higher consciousness. And then don't ever lie to me again, Marian.

MARIAN: This is not like you, Ralph.

MARIAN *starts the dryer.*

RALPH: What? To demand? You're right, Marian, but I want to know. I want to know the truth.

MARIAN: We're just talking, right?

RALPH: Yes, Marian. We're just talking.

MARIAN: You want me to tell you the truth.

RALPH: That's all I've ever asked, Marian.

She continues to dry her skirt with the hair dryer.

MARIAN: Okay, he kissed me. Does that satisfy you?

RALPH: Did that satisfy you?

MARIAN: Everybody was pretty far gone, as you may or may not remember.

RALPH: I don't really need all this perspective. Just the facts.

MARIAN *picks up the skirt in one hand and the hair dryer in the other. She stands in front of* RALPH *naked from the waist down, drying her skirt.*

MARIAN: All right. All right, Ralph. Okay. Somehow the two of us were elected to go out and get liquor. We drove to Foremost, which was closed, and then Cappy's, which was also closed. In fact, everything was closed. And I was beginning to wonder whether anything would be open. All I could think of were those all-night supermarkets. I wondered whether anyone would even be in the mood for a drink if we had to drive around half the night looking for an open market.

She continues drying her skirt.

MARIAN: He was really drunk. I hadn't even realized how drunk he was until we started driving. He was terribly slow and all hunched over the wheel and we were talking about a lot of things, a lot of things that didn't make sense . . . about religious images and this painter named Larry Rivers and then he said something about Norman Mailer and about how Norman Mailer stabbed his wife in the breast. And he said he'd hate it if anybody did that to me. He said he'd like to kiss my breast. And then he pulled the car over to the side of the road and then he kissed me.

MARIAN *finishes drying her shirt and shuts off the hair dryer. She walks back to the table and spreads out the skirt.*

RALPH: How long?

MARIAN: How long, what?

RALPH: How long did he kiss you?

MARIAN *is either thinking or doesn't want to answer.*

RALPH: Then what?

MARIAN: Then he said do you want to have a go at it?

RALPH: Jesus, Marian. Do you want to have a go at it? Do you want to have a go at it? Do you want to have a go at it?! What does that mean, Marian? Do you want to have a go at it? Did he kiss your tits? Did you touch him?

MARIAN: Touch him? Touch him? Okay, Ralph, you want to know what happened? He kissed me and I kissed him back.

MARIAN *pulls on her skirt furiously.*

MARIAN: And then we did it. We just did it right there in the car. He fucked me right there in the car. I was drunk. It didn't mean anything to me. I wish it hadn't happened, but it did. Is that all you want to know? Is that all? Is that all?

RALPH: Yes, Marian. That's all.

RALPH *gets up and begins walking out of the room.*

MARIAN: Ralph, he didn't come in me. I swear to God, he didn't come in me.

RALPH: Okay.

MARIAN: Where are you going, Ralph?

RALPH: Well, Marian, we have guests coming. I'm gonna go and light the barbecue.

He opens the door. We see the light from the outside.

INT—THE LOW NOTE—LATE DAY

We see the light from the outside as ZOE *opens the door to the jazz club.* ZOE *carries her cello. She seems very shy. We hear* TESS *rehearsing "I Don't Want to Cry Anymore."*

JAY, *the bartender, comes over to* ZOE.

JAY: We're closed. Can I help you?

ZOE: I just came to talk to my mom.

JAY: Who's your mom?

ZOE *points to* TESS. ZOE *picks up her cello and walks to the bar.* JERI *walks over to* JAY.

JERI: Who's that?

JAY: She said she's Tess' kid.

JERI: You're kiddin'. A string player?

TESS *sees* ZOE. *She puts down the microphone and comes over to the bar.*

TESS: What're you doin' here, Zoe?

ZOE: Mom, Casey died.

TESS: Casey? Who's that?

ZOE: The little boy. Lives right next door. He got run over by a car.

TESS *keeps looking back at the stage trying to monitor both conversations.*

TESS: I'll be damned. Just like that. Kids.

ZOE: I just saw Mrs. Finnigan. I feel so bad for them. I thought you'd want to know.

ZOE *puts her hand on* TESS' *shoulder.*

TESS: It's a cryin' shame, baby. She must feel like shit.

ZOE: Mom?

TESS: Why don't you go sit down over there. We're just rehearsing.

TESS *starts back to the stage.*

ZOE: Mom?

TESS *picks up the rehearsal where she left off.* ZOE *waits for a moment then walks out of the club.*

EXT—SHEPARD HOUSE—LATE DAY

GENE *rides up on his motorcycle with* SUZY *in the saddlebag.* SANDY, WILL, *and* AUSTIN *are playing in the front yard. They run up to* GENE.

SANDY: Suzy! Suzy! Daddy you brought Suzy back.

SANDY *takes* SUZY *out. The kids are very happy.* SHERRI *comes out of the house and over to* GENE. *The kids are occupied with* SUZY.

SANDY: I missed you, Suzy.

AUSTIN: Daddy, why can't I have a monkey?

GENE *and* SHERRI *kiss.*

EXT/INT—WYMAN HOUSE—LATE DAY

STUART *and* CLAIRE, *in the Clownmobile, pull up in front of the Wyman's house.* STUART *carries the trout.*

STUART: Jesus, I hate this goddamn thing.

CLAIRE: Well if you'd get a job you could get your own car fixed.

STUART: Sure this is the right address? Huh?

INT—WYMAN HOUSE—LATE DAY

>   MARIAN *goes to the door when the Kanes ring.* RALPH *is at the bar.*

CLAIRE: Hi.
MARIAN: Come in.
CLAIRE: We're not early, are we?
MARIAN: No, not at all. Did you have any trouble finding the house?
STUART: Not at all. I got the fish. Where should I put this?
MARIAN: Come on in.

>   RALPH *is mixing drinks. The TV is on.*

MARIAN: Ralph . . . *(to* CLAIRE*)* You want a drink?

>   RALPH *hands her one.*

CLAIRE: Oh, thank you.
MARIAN: Let's go to the patio.

>   *The women walk off.* STUART *sets the fish container on the bar.*

STUART: How are you?
RALPH: Hello Steven.
STUART: Stuart.
RALPH: Right, sorry.

>   *CAMERA turns to* CLAIRE *admiring the paintings.*

CLAIRE: Oh, wow, look at those pictures. Where'd you get them?
MARIAN: They're mine. I painted them.
CLAIRE: You're kidding.

>   *They walk out to the patio.*

>   *CAMERA turns to* RALPH *and* STUART *at the bar. We see* MARIAN *and* CLAIRE *through the window looking at the view.*

RALPH: How was the trip?
STUART: Not bad. We took the 405 to the 10 . . .
RALPH: No, I meant the fishing trip.
STUART: Oh. It was great. *(picks up fish)* Got it right here. Want me to take it to the kitchen or something?
RALPH: Oh, why don't we just take it right out to the barbecue.

>   RALPH *leads the way to the patio.*

RALPH: You like fishing?
STUART: Oh, I love to fish.

RALPH: Is that your hobby? Fishing?

STUART: Well, not really. I enjoy it though. But I don't like fishing in boats. 'Cause I don't swim. So I don't like fishing on lakes or the ocean.

The women are starting back into the house.

MARIAN: I'll give you the tour. Start with the upstairs first. Show you the bed-rooms first.

CAMERA PANS to JEOPARDY game box. We hear the men on the patio. Their conversation trails off.

RALPH: So where do you fish mostly?

STUART: Different places. I don't get out as much as I'd like. What about you? You a fisherman?

INT—STONE APARTMENT—NIGHT

We see the aquarium then HONEY. *She's the picture of a battered woman, swollen and bloodied. She turns away and we see* BILL *who looks sullen and brutish. We hear what sounds like a slap and* HONEY *sprawls on the bed.*

BILL: I'm sorry I had to do that but you just got outta line.

HONEY: Come on, Bill.

BILL: I know I'm just the gardener—.

HONEY: *(laughs)* I'm gettin' tired of this.

BILL *on his knees straddles* HONEY. *He raises his fist like he's going to punch her.*

BILL: Oh, no, let me fix this for you.

He picks up a brush and begins to touch up the blood around her mouth. She starts to squirm.

BILL: Don't.

HONEY: Bill, this is takin' fucking hours.

BILL: Yeah, well, you know. Stop it. Stop it don't move.

HONEY: I gotta go to the bathroom. Don't lean on me like that. I'm takin' this thing out too.

HONEY *takes the lump out of her mouth.*

BILL: No, just keep it in for the picture.

HONEY: Hold it. Just a second.

BILL: Support your husband.

BILL *takes his camera and begins focusing on her.*

BILL: Now look like someone really hurt you. Like Earl beat you up.

HONEY: Shut up.

BILL: Did he?

HONEY: You know he didn't.

BILL: I know he didn't literally, but what else did he do? What do you think about when you think about Earl?

HONEY: Can we stop, Bill? I don't want to talk about that, okay? Come on, Bill, let's get goin'.

BILL: I'm in the shower sometimes and I hear water running down the drain and I think it's someone hurting you in the other room. And it scares me.

HONEY: Bill.

BILL: Open your top a little for this.

HONEY: Bill, I don't wanna do this.

BILL: Come on.

HONEY: I don't wanna do this anymore. I been very patient.

BILL: I could speed up the process—. *(smacking his fist in his hand)*

HONEY: No.

BILL: I coulda just done my quick version. Crunch! Crack!

HONEY: *(laughing)* Please.

BILL: But I didn't 'cause I love you so.

HONEY: I love you too.

BILL: Why did that excite me so? I started to get a little chubby when I was doing that. That's weird.

> BILL *takes out a butcher knife and holds it like a weapon.*

BILL: Okay this's my last request.

HONEY: That's it. I'm gettin' restless.

> *He puts the butcher knife under her armpit.*

HONEY: This is it. I been a good sport.

> BILL *stands up with the camera.*

BILL: Just hold this. You're dead and your husband is a creep.

HONEY: Do it, do it, I'm ready.

BILL: *(squeaky voice)* I love you.

EXT—WYMAN HOUSE/PATIO—NIGHT

> MARIAN *sets up the game Jeopardy.* RALPH *is mixing drinks. It seems very relaxed.*

STUART: I'm in sales. Hardware primarily. But I've sold everything else.

CLAIRE: Clothes.

STUART: I never sold clothes.

CLAIRE: That's what I'm saying. Everything but clothes.

RALPH: So you're retired?

MARIAN: Oh, you know what, I'm almost set up. Ralph, could you bring everybody over.

RALPH *leads* CLAIRE *to her seat.* STUART *follows them.*

STUART: I've been out of work three months now. Nobody seems too be interested in salesmen anymore.

RALPH *is not listening to* STUART. *He's thinking about* MARIAN. *He walks around to* MARIAN.

MARIAN: Could you sit over there.

RALPH: *(leaning down)* Are you gonna be Alex Tra-bick?

MARIAN: Yes I gonna be Alex Trebek. Well, on that note, why don't we go ahead and start the game. Claire, you want to pick a category: The Night Skies, Political Quotes, Racy Movies, the Blues.

CLAIRE: Oh, racy movies, racy movies.

INT—KAISER HOUSE—NIGHT

LOIS *is on the couch talking on the phone in her sexy voice.*

LOIS: Oh, yeah, right on my clit.

She leans forward and picks up a magazine off the coffee table and begins flipping through the pages as she talks.

LOIS: And now take your fingers and put 'em inside me, oh yeah, just fuck me with your fingers, baby . . .

JERRY *walks out of* JOE'S *room and closes the door.*

LOIS: Don't you want to go inside? You want to hear how wet I am for you.

LOIS *puts her fingers in her mouth and simulates the sound she just described.* JERRY *is looking for something on the coffee table.* LOIS *covers the phone.*

LOIS: *(to* JERRY*)* What are you doin'?

JERRY: Getting a roach.

LOIS: *(to caller)* That's how wet you make my pussy, baby. Oooh, I really want you to fuck me now. I want you to go inside me with your big, hard cock. Oh, wait, wait. Make me beg for it. Just tease my clit, please baby. Oh my legs are spread so wide . . .

LOIS *is matter-of-factly massaging her toes and still looking at the magazine.* JERRY *stands in the door listening to* LOIS.

LOIS: Oh, I feel you fucking me so deep, oh please harder, harder. Oh, I can feel your balls against my ass, baby. Oh, yeah. Lift my legs above your shoulders. Oh, fuck me so hard. Oh, I'm gonna come. Oh . . .

Her expression changes. She's been hung up on. LOIS *puts down the phone, checks her watch and writes in her log book.*

JERRY: Sounded like you got really hot talkin' to that guy.
LOIS: Yeah, right. You give Joe-Joe his ear drops?
JERRY: Talkin' about his dick and everything.
LOIS: Dick? I never say that word.
JERRY: Cock. Whatever.
LOIS: I hate that word. Dick.

EXT/INT—TRAINER HOUSE/GARAGE—NIGHT

ZOE *drives into the garage. The door closes but her car is still running. She takes her cello case out and lays it down on the garage floor. She opens it. By now we see exhaust fumes.*

EXT—WYMAN HOUSE/PATIO—NIGHT

The barbecue is smoking. CLAIRE, STUART, *and* RALPH *are playing Jeopardy.*

RALPH: Who is Mariette Hartley.
MARIAN: That's right.
STUART: Well who is Mariette Hartley?
RALPH: It's not really fair that I should win all the time.
MARIAN: Are you cheating, Ralph?
RALPH: No, Marian. You cheat, remember?
CLAIRE: *(Laughing)* Ooooh.
MARIAN: All right this time you be Alex Trebek, okay? Time to switch.
CLAIRE: All right, Stuart, you have to sit in the middle.

They all get up and move. RALPH *passes* MARIAN.

RALPH: Does Alex Trebek cheat?

STUART *grabs* CLAIRE *around the waist. Her smile quickly vanishes. She's not in the mood.*

RALPH: Hey, hey, hey, hey!

STUART *lets* CLAIRE *go.*

STUART: Here are the categories: Little songs, Celebrities, Gourmet cooking, Family life. *(suddenly remembering)* Gourmet cooking. Shit!

> RALPH *rushes over to the barbecue and opens the lid. There's a lot of laughter and merriment when everyone sees the burning fish.*

RALPH: Shit! I thought you said ten minutes an inch, Stuart.
STUART: I did. The thickness, not the length.
RALPH: How about we have another Piña Colada?

INT—TRAINER HOUSE/GARAGE—NIGHT

> ZOE *sits on a box playing the cello. It is eerie. The car is still running.*

INT—THE LOW NOTE—NIGHT

> TESS *is singing "I Don't Know You".*

TESS: "You may mean me some good. You may mean me some harm. You may be a fire. You may be a false alarm. I don't know you. I don't know you. I don't know you."

INT—KAISER HOUSE/BEDROOOM—NIGHT

> LOIS *and* JERRY *walk in the bedroom.* LOIS *starts to undress for bed.*

JERRY: I don't think you should talk in front of the kids like that.
LOIS: They don't understand.
JERRY: How do you know?
LOIS: Goes in one ear and goes out the other. You should be happy I have a job where I'm home all the time, you know, instead of some funky day care. And I make damn good money. Did you collect from Ryan's yet? I don't want you servicing their pool again until they pay you.
JERRY: How come you don't ever talk to me like that?
LOIS: Like what?
JERRY: Like the way you talk those guys off.
LOIS: Are you kidding me?
JERRY: It might spice things up.
LOIS: Look, you wanna fuck me, fuck me. I'm just a little talked out, you know.

> LOIS *can't unfasten her bracelet.*

LOIS: Shit. Could you get this for me?

JERRY *tries to unfasten her bracelet.*

LOIS: Jerry, big bear. Did I hurt your feelings? Look at me.
JERRY: No.
LOIS: Look at me.
JERRY: It's all right. Let me just get this.
LOIS: I'm so glad Joe-Joe got your eyes. You wanna fuck? Hmmm? Yeah, let's fuck. Come on we can fuck.

They start to kiss. JERRY *is suddenly in the mood.* LOIS *stops.*

LOIS: Oh, shit, I forgot. The TV.

JERRY *waits but she doesn't return. He takes off his watch and throws it on the night table. He turns off the light.*

EXT—WYMAN HOUSE/PATIO—NIGHT

MARIAN *and* CLAIRE *come down the spiral staircase both dressed in clown suits.*

MARIAN and CLAIRE: *(singing)* "My little puppy's name is Rags,
He eats so much that his tummy sags.
His ears flip-flop and his tail wig-wags,
he walks back and forth in a big zig-zag.
He doesn't have any pedigree.
But I love him, and he loves me.
Flip-flop, wig-wag, zig-zag . . . "

As their song continues we hear STUART *and* RALPH.

STUART: You being a doctor and all, do you touch many dead bodies?
RALPH: That's kind of a strange question isn't it, Stuart?
CLAIRE: Come on! It's your turn. A little makeup, little costuming, weird behavior. Isn't that what it's all about? Don't look at me like that, Stuart. It's always me underneath, you know. I can change, but I can always go back to me.
RALPH: Marian, what do you got on underneath?
MARIAN: You know, Ralph. Nothing!
CLAIRE: *(to* RALPH*)* What do you want to be?
RALPH: I wanna be nothing!
MARIAN: *(to* STUART*)* I'm gonna make you a pussy . . . cat.
STUART: Does this stuff come off?
MARIAN: Oh, sure.
CLAIRE: *(to* RALPH*)* Well, I know how to do nothing. We'll just erase your face.

CLAIRE *sits on* RALPH'S *lap.*

CLAIRE: *(sings)* "In a setting by the woods.
A little man by the river stood.
Saw a girl come floating by,
and he heard her cry.
Help me, help me,
help me she said—."
STUART: But he couldn't help her, she was dead.

INT—FINNIGAN HOUSE/BEDROOM—NIGHT

ANN *wakes up with a sudden revelation.*

ANN: I know who it was. The baker. Casey's birthday cake.

ANN *sits straight up.*

ANN: Howard?
HOWARD: What? What is it?
ANN: I know who made the phone calls.
HOWARD: Who?
ANN: The baker, Mr. Bitkower.

HOWARD *puts his arms around* ANN. *She shakes him off.*

ANN: Stop it. Don't do that.

INT—THE LOW NOTE—NIGHT

TESS *sings "I Don't Know You".*

TESS: "I don't know you well. I don't know you at all. I don't know you. I don't know you. I don't know you."

EXT—WYMAN HOUSE—PATIO—SUNRISE

CLAIRE *is waking up on the chaise, yawning. As the CAMERA PULLS BACK we see balloons tied in the shape of animals.* RALPH *with clown face is blowing up balloons using a helium tank.* STUART *is trying to sketch* MARIAN.

STUART: You know my mother was an artist, sort of. She always said I should or I could. But I don't know.
MARIAN: When I was in art school, I had a teacher. He eventually killed himself. Couldn't sell anything. But he'd have us paint with sticks, rocks, whatever you could find, like cavemen or something. I guess is what it was supposed to be like. Never allowed brushes or pencils or real paint—paint you could buy anyway. It was to get you to feel or something. I've forgotten.

The CAMERA turns to RALPH. *Pinching the ends of the balloon, he lets out the air making a high-pitched scream. He makes a face that goes with the scream until the balloon flies out of his hand.*

INT—TRAINER HOUSE—DAWN

TESS *pulls in the driveway, gets out, and starts for the front door. She hears an engine and sees the exhaust seeping out. She pounds on the garage door.*

TESS: Zoe! Zoe, don't do this to me. Zoe!

TESS *goes to her car for the door opener. As the door raises a haze of exhaust begins to clear.* ZOE *is lying on the floor.*
TESS *screams and runs to* ZOE.

TESS: No! Oh, baby, no!

EXT/INT—BAKERY—DAY

We see ANN *pounding on the glass doors.* HOWARD *is trying to look inside. Finally* ANDY BITKOWER *comes out from the back room.*

ANDY: I'm not open yet. The bakery is closed for business.

He turns and leaves while ANN *is still talking.*

ANN: We can see that you're closed, but I'm sure you'll see us, Mr. Bitkower. Mr. Bitkower.

INT—BAKERY—DAY

ANDY *is thinking about the couple.* HOWARD *pushes the back door open. This catches* ANDY *off-guard.*

ANDY: Hey, you're not allowed in here.
ANN: Mr. Bitkower.
ANDY: What do you want?
ANN: I'm Casey's mother, and this is Casey's father.
ANDY: I'm busy. You come back when I'm open.
ANN: No.
ANDY: All right. You want your cake now. Is that it? You finally want the cake you ordered?
HOWARD: Wanna talk about the cake that wasn't picked up?
ANDY: Or paid for.
ANN: You're a terrible person, Mr. Bitkower.

ANDY: It cost me time and money to make that cake. I have work to do. I don't want to talk to you.

HOWARD: Well you're gonna talk to her, or I'm gonna knock you on your ass, pal.

ANN: How can you be so cheap and insensitive?

ANDY: Lady, I work 16 hours a day to make ends meet. I have to get back to work. I bake all night and work all day.

ANN: You bake all night? Ha! I thought you made phone calls at night, you bastard.

ANDY: I'm going to call somebody. You get out of my store.

ANN looks so threatening that ANDY actually picks up a bread paddle. HOWARD grabs it out of his hand and flings it away.

ANDY: I don't want any trouble here.

ANN: My son's dead. He is dead, Mr. Bitkower. He was hit by a car the day I ordered the cake. We've been waiting with him in the hospital until he died. Now he's dead. There are no more birthdays. He's dead, you bastard———.

She starts to hit ANDY hard with her fists, but he has gone limp at what she just said.

ANN: You bastard! Goddamn you! Goddamn you! Goddamn you!

HOWARD restrains her. ANN cries uncontrollably. He starts to lead her away. ANDY is too stunned to speak.

HOWARD: Shame on you. Shame on you.

ANDY watches for a moment.

ANDY: Oh, this is terrible. Wait. Don't go. Wait.

ANDY closes the back door.

ANDY: Please sit down. Let me get you a chair.

He brings up two chairs.

ANDY: Please, sit down, both of you.

ANDY puts his arms on ANN. She holds him and sobs.

EXT—ONE-HOUR PHOTO—DAY

The KAISERS and the BUSHES are piled in JERRY'S COOL POOL SERVICE truck as it pulls into a convenience store parking lot next to the ONE HOUR PHOTO. The adults pile out.

LOIS: Josette stay in the car. Joe-Joe, watch your sister.

BILL *and* JERRY *head for the convenience store.*

BILL: You want anything?

LOIS: Cigarettes.

HONEY: Beer. Lots of beer.

JOE: Where you goin'?

LOIS: We're goin' to get Aunt Honey's photographs. You watch Josette.

> LOIS *and* HONEY *stand at the kiosk waiting.* GORDON JOHNSON *walks up to the window and leans down to show his ticket to the* CLERK.

CLERK: Hi, Mr. Johnson! How's it goin'? Here you are.

> *In the exchange of money and pictures both sets of pictures get knocked on the ground.* HONEY *takes hers.* GORDON *takes his. As they walk away they each open their pictures. We see* HONEY *and* LOIS *first looking at* GORDON'S *fishing pictures. They both gasp when they see the dead body the fishermen found.*
> GORDON *opens his and shuffles through the pictures of what looks like a dead woman in bed. He flips up his glasses and looks at the women.*
> *Without a word* HONEY *and* GORDON *walk towards each other and exchange pictures.*
> HONEY *and* LOIS *repeat the license plate number of* GORDON'S *car.*

HONEY: Remember 7NZ699. 7NZ699.

JERRY: Come on. Get in. We gonna do this picnic or what?

> *As they climb in,* HONEY *and* LOIS *are still repeating Gordon's license number to themselves.*

HONEY & LOIS: 7NZ699.

> GORDON *gets into his car repeating the phone number on Jerry's truck.*

GORDON: 604-8364. 604-8364.

INT—PIGGOT TRAILER—DAY

> DOREEN *and* EARL *are sitting on the couch. They both have Hawaiian leis around their necks. They are both drinking and enjoying each other.* DOREEN *reaches for an hors d'oeuvre from a plate on the coffee table and feeds it to* EARL.

EARL: So look what you do. You make the food look like a little show down there on the plate. Like a little stage with little sausage people. So cute.

> DOREEN *laughs. She loves it.*

EARL: I love all those things about you.

DOREEN: And I love everything you say.

They kiss.

EARL: I'm gettin' us out of Downey, baby. Don't worry about it. It's temporary.

EXT—L.A. STREETS—DAY

> BETTY WEATHERS *is in a red Mustang convertible driven by* WALLY LITTLETON, *an airline pilot.* CHAD *is in the back seat.*

BETTY: Oh, I don't want it to be over.
WALLY: We'll do it again.
BETTY: When?
WALLY: Well I got three round trips out of JFK to Berlin. Then stopover in Bangkok, four-day layover that I requested. That'll be great. So, next month. Maybe we should go to Hawaii. Chad could stay with his father. I mean he'll be in school, right?
BETTY: Chad had a great time.
WALLY: Wally had a great time.
BETTY: How 'bout 'Little Wally'.
WALLY: Smokin' good time.

> BETTY *laughs hard.*

WALLY: Yippee-Yi-Yah.

EXT—PARK AREA—DAY

> JERRY *drives his El Camino down a service road into the park and past other picnickers and smoking barbecues. As everyone climbs out we hear:*

HONEY: Watch out for the dog shit.

INT—PIGGOT TRAILER—DAY

> EARL *and* DOREEN *are drinking and having fun.* EARL *is singing and doing a little dance. They both have maraccas.*

EARL: Gettin' outta Downey.
DOREEN: Take me outta Downey.
EARL: I'm ona getcha outta Downey.
DOREEN: Take me outta Downey.

> DOREEN *starts laughing too hard to sing.*

EARL: Gettin' outta Downey.

> *They both collapse in laughter.*

EXT—PICNIC AREA—DAY

The picnic is in full swing. JERRY *and* BILL *play baseball with* JOE. LOIS *and* HONEY *are talking and watching* JOSETTE, *who suddenly breaks and runs away.* LOIS *chases her.*

LOIS: Oh, big girly.

She picks JOSETTE *up and swings her around.*

LOIS: Such a wild thing.

BARBARA *and* NANCY *try to ride their bicycles down a slope too steep for them.* NANCY *runs into* JERRY'S *truck at the bottom, but not hard.* BILL *and* JERRY *stop playing baseball.* BILL *is immediately interested.*

BILL: Okay?
BARBARA & NANCY: Yeah.
BILL: How's the car?
NANCY: Fine.

The girls smile and ride off.

BILL: Have a nice day.

JOE *chases after the girls hitting their tires with a baseball bat.*

LOIS & HONEY: Joe! Leave those girls alone.
LOIS: Just like his dad. Totally outta control.

BILL *and* JERRY *watch the girls ride out of sight.*

BILL: How'd you like a little of that stickin' on your drop shoot? Ten bucks says they're waitin' for us. Let's go.
JERRY: Okay.

BILL *and* JERRY *walk over to the cooler.*

BILL: Honey, Honey.

He indicates with his fingers to his lips that they are going to go smoke a joint.

BILL: Be back in five.
HONEY: Okay. Would you hand me a beer?
LOIS: Where're you goin'?
BILL: We're gonna go . . . *(fingers to lips)* Discretion around the little ones.

BILL *and* JERRY *each take a couple beers. The women are distracted.*

LOIS: *(to* JOE*)* Ow. Don't hit me!

BILL *and* JERRY *trot off in the direction the girls were last seen.* LOIS *and* HONEY *start to prepare food.*

LOIS: We have baloney. We have swiss cheese. We have peanut butter . . .

INT—BAKERY—DAY

ANDY *carries a tray of muffins over to* ANN *and* HOWARD.

ANDY: Here, eat these. You need to eat something to keep going. Eating is a good thing at a time like this. I hope you like my muffins.

ANN *and* HOWARD *begin to eat.*

ANN: Mr. Bitkower?
ANDY: Yes, Mrs. Finnigan, what can I get you?
ANN: I'd like to see the cake.

ANDY *stands with his back to her for a long time. And then:*

ANDY: You can't. I threw it away.

EXT—BETTY'S HOUSE—DAY

WALLY *pulls up in front of the house.*

BETTY: Okay, here we are. Let's go, Chad.

CHAD *climbs out.*

WALLY: Don't forget these, bud.

CHAD *ignores him.* BETTY *takes the bag of toys from* WALLY. *She walks around to* WALLY'S *and gives him a kiss.*

CHAD: Bye, Gene.
BETTY: Wally. Wally. Bye, Wally.

WALLY *drives off.* BETTY *and* CHAD *walk towards the house.*

BETTY: Ah, home sweet home.
CHAD: Really.

When BETTY *opens the door she's too stunned to speak.* CHAD *sees a business card on his Tinker Toy structure.*

CHAD: Aubrey Bell? Mommy, who's Aubrey Bell?

BETTY *doesn't answer. She can't.* CHAD *gets interested in "Captain Planet" on television. He sits down on the clean carpet to watch, oblivious to the destruction around him.*

EXT—MOUNTAINS/PICNIC AREA—DAY

BARBARA *and* NANCY *peddle along the road then turn off onto a dirt trail.* BILL *and* JERRY *come into view not far behind.*

JERRY: They're on bikes.
BILL: No, no, no. They gotta cut through here. They gotta cut through here.
JERRY: I don't wanna run all over these mountains for a couple of cockteasers.

NANCY *and* BARBARA *discover that the trail is a dead end.*

NANCY: Look's like we're stopping here.
BARBARA: Those guys are following us.

BILL *and* JERRY *approach.*

BILL: I'll warm 'em up and you just come in on what I say. *(to* BARBARA *and* NANCY*)* Hey, how are you?
BARBARA: Okay.
BILL: Hey, I know you.
BARBARA: No.
BILL: From . . . Sure I do. From the the photo shoot. I did your makeup.
BARBARA: I don't know what you're talking about.
BILL: From the photo shoot. I'm a makeup artist. And I thought you were someone I'd done for a shoot.

BARBARA *and* NANCY *look at each other and laugh.*

BILL: Is that funny.
NANCY: Sorry.
BILL: Are you guys actresses or models?
NANCY: We're not either. I'm not . . . we're not either one.
BILL: You're not? I just mean . . . 'cause you have the looks for it. I think you could be, you know, if you wanted to.
BARBARA: Well, if it happened, that'd be okay. If it doesn't happen, that's okay too.
BILL: But, hey, sometimes I do some talent scout stuff too. I mean if you ever wanted to . . . I'm Bill. This is Jerry.
JERRY: Want a beer?
NANCY: No thanks.
BARBARA: No.
NANCY: So have you done any movie stars?
BILL: Yeah. Yes, ma'am.

NANCY: Really? Who's the biggest star you've done?

BILL: *(to* JERRY*)* Yeah, what was that one? What was the last one I did? Who was that big one I did last time?

JERRY seems to be in a daze.

BILL: I think it was Roseanne Barr.

The girls laugh.

BILL: She's big. She's huge.

NANCY: You're lying. I can tell you're lying.

BILL: Yeah, that didn't work. What's your name?

BARBARA: Barbara. And that's Nancy.

NANCY: So you married?

JERRY: No.

BILL: We were. Very unfortunate.

BARBARA: I'll have one of those beers.

BILL: You know what's 100 yards from you? You know the Bat Caves? You ever watch Batman? 'Member the series Batman? Well, the Bat Caves where they shot . . . let me just show you this cave. *(to* NANCY*)* Let me take Barbara away from you for just one second.

BARBARA: I'll just have one beer.

NANCY: One.

BILL pats JERRY'S *shoulder answering* NANCY.

BILL: Don't worry about it.

NANCY: Come back.

BILL and BARBARA *walk towards the main road.*

NANCY: Can I have a beer?

JERRY gives NANCY *a beer. When she opens the can it spews out, soaking her.* NANCY *turns away from* JERRY.

NANCY: Do you mind?

NANCY starts to remove her shirt. She is wearing a blue bra underneath. JERRY *watches her.*
BARBARA and BILL *are walking and talking, and then they hear* NANCY *in trouble.*

NANCY: What are you doing? What?! Ah! Stop it!

BARBARA and BILL *turn, and at that moment* JERRY *is clubbing* NANCY *with a*

128

rock. There is a rumble, a group of birds flying off in all directions, the sound of falling rocks. It is an earthquake. BARBARA and BILL lose their balance. JERRY stands looking around. His face is spattered with blood. NANCY is on the ground dead.

EXT—PICNIC AREA—DAY

LOIS, HONEY, and the KIDS react to the earthquake. They scream wondering where the men are:

LOIS: Jerry? Jerry!

INT—BAKERY—DAY

Metal bowls and baking sheets are falling all around them. ANN and HOWARD react but don't know what to do.

ANDY: I think, under the table.

They all get under the table.

EXT/INT—SHEPARD HOUSE—DAY

SHERRI is picking up the KIDS' toys on the patio. The earthquake begins. She drops everything in her arms and gathers the KIDS.

SHERRI: Gene! Gene! Earthquake!

GENE runs past her shouting:

GENE: Underneath the door!

GENE stands on the patio with an LAPD bullhorn:

GENE: This is Officer Gene Shepard of the Los Angeles Police Department. We are currently experiencing an earthquake.

INT—TRAINER HOUSE/ZOE'S REHEARSAL ROOM—DAY

TESS is in ZOE's room. She seems unaware of the earthquake as she sings "Conversation On A Barstool".

TESS: ". . . On Broadway I danced for that Senator.
They know me in London, they know me in Paris . . ."

ZOE's cello falls over on the floor.

EXT—WYMAN HOUSE/PATIO—DAY

CLAIRE, STUART, MARIAN *and* RALPH *are in the jacuzzi.*

STUART: Don't worry. Don't worry! It's not the big one.

INT—BETTY'S HOUSE—DAY

BETTY *and* CHAD *are already surrounded by wreckage.* BETTY *starts laughing hysterically.* CHAD *is in charge. He makes her crouch down on the floor.*

CHAD: Just wait it out, mommy.

BETTY *laughs hysterically when* STORMY*'s clock falls and smashes.*

INT/EXT—PIGGOT MOBILE HOME—DAY

DOREEN *and* EARL *are laughing as they make their way to a doorway.*

EXT/INT—SHEPARD HOUSE—DAY

SHERRI *is huddled with the kids.* GENE *is on the bullhorn:*

GENE: If you are close in proximity to any power lines, please move quickly away as falling power lines can result in electrocution. Due to the possibility of ruptured gas lines . . . .

INT—PIGGOT TRAILER—DAY

DOREEN *and* EARL *stand in the doorway.*

EARL: This is The Big One, baby, we're goin' out together.

They kiss and laugh.

EARL: This is The Big One, baby.

The shaking stops.

DOREEN: *(sipping her drink)* Wasn't The Big One.

They laugh about this too.

INT—BAKERY—DAY

> ANN, HOWARD, *and* ANDY *come out from under the table.* ANN *breaths a sigh of relief.*

EXT—PICNIC AREA—DAY

> HONEY *and* LOIS *are still looking around for the men.* LOIS *holds* JOSETTE.

LOIS: *(kissing* JOSETTE*)* Such a brave boy. Where the fuck are they? JERRY!

EXT/INT—SHEPARD HOUSE—DAY

> GENE *comes over to his family in the doorway, puts his arms around* SHERRI *and the kids and pulls them close to him.*

EXT—WYMAN HOUSE—DAY

> *The* WYMANS *and* KANES *climb out of the jacuzzi.*

MARIAN: We should probably eat is what we should do.
STUART: Yeah what happened to that big meal we were supposed to have?
MARIAN: We should probably have a whole bunch of eggs or something.
CLAIRE: We should probably turn on the TV.
MARIAN: I'm gonna make a whole bunch of eggs.

INT—TRAINER HOUSE—DAY

> TESS *hums the melody of "Conversation On A Barstool". She is trancelike.*

INT—WYMAN HOUSE—DAY

> *Anchorman* JERRY DUNPHY *is on the TV:*

JERRY DUNPHY: Fifteen people have been injured and we're told one person died
. . .
STUART: One person killed.
CLAIRE: One fatatality. *(shrugging)* Well, you know, that's not really so bad. One person.
JERRY DUNPHY: We go live now to Santa Monica airport where Stormy Weathers has just landed. Stormy was in the air when the quake happened. Stormy, tell us exactly what you saw.

No one is paying real close attention but we manage to hear the gist of what Stormy is saying.

STORMY: As I was landing I was thinking to myself what a beautiful sight L.A. is.
STUART: Do you have any bourbon?
RALPH: How about some Tequila?
ALL: Yeah.
STORMY: It is a beautiful day, the kind of day every Angelino says to himself or herself just how lucky he or she is to be living in L.A. Back to you, Jerry.

MARIAN, STUART, *and* CLAIRE *walk outside to the patio bar. We hear* JERRY DUNPHY:

JERRY DUNPHY: Now here is the latest news on the earthquake. There is one fatality. This has been confirmed now. A young woman in Griffith Park was killed by falling rocks. Appparently while hiking. We're not sure yet if the death was earthquake related. Sixty people have been treated at area hospitals . . . .
RALPH: Here's to lemonade.
MARIAN: Lemonade.

They all toast, lick the salt on the backs of their hands, throw back the Tequila, and suck the lemons. They all make a sour face.

As the CAMERA PANS off of the four the music comes up. TESS *sings "Prisoner of Life." CAMERA continues to move across the patio and then to the sweeping view of L.A.*

END

Ann Finnigan	ANDIE MacDOWELL
Howard Finnigan	BRUCE DAVISON
Paul Finnigan	JACK LEMMON
Casey Finnigan	ZANE CASSIDY
Marian Wyman	JULIANNE MOORE
Dr. Ralph Wyman	MATTHEW MODINE
Claire Kane	ANNE ARCHER
Stuart Kane	FRED WARD
Lois Kaiser	JENNIFER JASON LEIGH
Jerry Kaiser	CHRIS PENN
Joe Kaiser	JOSEPH C. HOPKINS
Josette Kaiser	JOSETTE MACCARIO
Honey Bush	LILI TAYLOR
Bill Bush	ROBERT DOWNEY, JR.
Sherri Shepard	MADELEINE STOWE
Gene Shepard	TIM ROBBINS
Sandy Shepard	CASSIE FRIEL
Will Shepard	DUSTIN FRIEL
Austin Shepard	AUSTIN FRIEL
Doreen Piggot	LILY TOMLIN
Earl Piggot	TOM WAITS
Betty Weathers	FRANCES McDORMAND
Stormy Weathers	PETER GALLAGHER
Chad Weathers	JARRETT LENNON
Tess Trainer	ANNIE ROSS
Zoe Trainer	LORI SINGER
Andy Bitkower	LYLE LOVETT
Gordon Johnson	BUCK HENRY
Vern Miller	HUEY LEWIS
Aubrey Bell	DANNY DARST
Dora Willis	MARGERIE BOND
Knute Willis	ROBERT DO'QUI
Joe Robbins	DARNELL WILLIAMS
Jim Stone	MICHAEL BEACH
Harriet Stone	ANDI CHAPMAN
Barbara	DEBORAH FALCONER
Nancy	SUSIE CUSACK
Wally Littleton	CHARLES ROCKET
Mrs. Schwartzmeier	JANE ALDEN

Jimmy Miller	CHRISTIAN ALTMAN
Jimmy's Friend	WILLIE MARLETT
Diner Customer	DIRK BLOCKER
Tarmac Secretary	SUZANNE CALVERT
Mourner	NATALIE STRONG
Bartender	JAY DELLA
Club Owner	JERUTH PERSSON
Joe Robbins' Pals	DEREK WEBSTER
	NATHANIEL H. HARRIS III
As Themselves	ALEX TREBEK
	JERRY DUNPHY

ANNIE ROSS & THE LOW NOTE QUINTET

Vocals	ANNIE ROSS
Piano	TERRY ADAMS
Drums	BOBBY PREVITE
Bass	GREG COHEN
Vibes	GENE ESTES
Trombone	BRUCE FOWLER

THE TROUT QUINTET

Cello	LORI SINGER
1st Violin	STUART CANIN
Violin	ANATOLY ROSINSKY
Viola	ROLAND KATO
Piano	ARMEN GUZELIMIAN

Marian's Paintings by	MEG FREEMAN
Associate Producers	MIKE KAPLAN
	DAVID LEVY
Unit Production Manager	DIANA POKORNY
First Assistant Director	ALLAN NICHOLLS
Second Assistant Director	JEFF RAFNER
Film Editor	SUZY ELMINGER
Art Director	JERRY FLEMING
Set Director	SUSAN J. EMSHWILLER
First Assistant Camera	ROBERT REED ALTMAN
Second Assistant Camera	BETH COTTER
Key Grip	ANTHONY T. MARRA II
Best Boy Grip	MICHAEL J. FAHEY
Dolly Grip	WAYNE STROUD
Grips	KEVIN J. FAHEY
	MICHAEL A. McFADDEN
	JAMES EARLEY

Gaffer	JACK ENGLISH
Best Boy Electric	JAMES BABINEAUX
Electricians	SCOTT GRAVES
	GEORGE M. CHAPPELL
	DANIEL MURPHY
	CHRISTOPHER LYONS
Location Managers	JACK KNEY
	PAUL D. BOYDSTON
Assistant Locations	CHRISTOPHER ARMSTRONG
Script Supervisor	LUCA KOUIMELIS
First Assistant Editors	DAVID LEONARD
	SANDRA KAUFMAN
Assistant Editors	DYLAN TICHENOR
	JEFFREY CRANFORD
Apprentice Editors	CHARLES COOPER
	JADE ALTMAN
Music Coordinator	SUSAN JACOBS
Music Recordist & Mixer	ERIC LILJESTRAND
Music Score Produced & Arranged by	MARK ISHAM
Recorded & Mixed by	STEPHEN KRAUSE
Performed by	DAVID SPELTZ & MARK ISHAM
Production Sound Mixer	JOHN PRITCHETT
Boom Operator	JOEL SHRYACK
Cable Puller	JOHN GLAESER
Make-Up/Hair Supervisor	THEO MAYES
Make-up/Hair	DEE DEE ALTAMURA
Wardrobe Supervisor	ANGELA BILLOWS
Wardrobe Assistants	AMY ENDRIES
	TIMOTHY A. WONSIK
Production Coordinator	SHELLY GLASSER
Assistant Coordinator	KRISTY HERR
Avenue Financial Representative	SHERI HALFON
Assistant to Robert Altman	JAMES McLINDON
Assistant to Cary Brokaw	DANIELLE KNIGHT
Sandcastle 5 Representative	CELIA CONVERSE
Property Master	ANTHONY MACCARIO
Assistant Property Master	WILLIAM MACCARIO
Second Assistant Props	JAMES FOLEY
Leadman	PETER BORCK

On Set Dresser	DAVID RONAN
Swing Gang	DANIEL ROTHENBERG
	RANDALL M. BOYD
	PETER R. EMSHWILLER
	JOSEPH GRAFMULLER
	KATE LONG
	RONALD D. PRICE, JR.
Scenic Paint Foreman	KELLY DECO
Assistant Painter	JAY G. SCHMIDT
Construction Coordinator	JOHN E. BUCKLIN
Construction Foreman	WAYNE SPRINGFIELD
Carpenters	DANIEL WHIFLER
	GORDON HOLMES
Art Department Coordinator	MICHELE GUASTELLO
Art Department Assistant	JOSHUA LUSBY
Still Photographer	JOYCE RUDOLPH
Research	SIGNE CORRIERE
Special Effects	JOHN HARRDIGAN
	CHRIS NELSON
Stunt Coordinator	GREG WALKER
Animal Trainer	KIM'S CRITTERS
Set Medic	JOSHUA W. BINDER
Helicopter Camera Operator	ALEXANDER WITT
Film Loader	CLAIRE M. SUTHERLAND
Supervising Sound Editor	ELIZA PALEY
Supervising Dialogue Editor	IRA SPIEGEL
Dialogue Editors	JEFFREY STERN
	ELLIOT DIETCH
Sound Effects Editor	MARGARET CRIMMINS
Foley Editor	MIRIAM BIDERMAN
Additional Sound Effects	PAUL P. SOUCEK
Additional Sound Editors	JULIE LINDNER
	ZEBORAH TIDWELL
Apprentice Sound Editors	GRETA GANDBHIR
	BARRY MALAWSKI
Intern	MARIO ONTAL
Re-Recording Mixer	LEE DICHTER
	MICHAEL BARRY
Foley Artist	ELISHA BIRNBAUM
Foley Recordist	GEORGE A. LARA
Additional Foleys	BRUCE PROSS
	FRANK KERN
	MARKO A. CONSTANZO

Production Assistants

ANGIE BONNER	NICK BERREAU
STEVEN DAY	TOM RUSS
SHANNON DOBSON	BRETT SCHLAMAN
TOYA HANKINS	CARL SHIMKIN
MICHAEL HUBERT	CORNELIUS SHULTZE-KRAFT
BARBARA WANSBROUGH	

Transportation Coordinator	DEREK RASER
Transportation Captain	J. T. THAYER II

Drivers

ALONZO BROWN, JR.	GIL HAYES
BRUCE CALLAHAN	DAVID JOSEPH
C. DAVID EARLE	WILLIAM MARK SPENCER
STEVE EARLE	EARL V. THIELEN
DON FEENEY	TRACY THIELEN
SCOTTY GOUDREAU	GREG WILLIS

Caterer	RICK BRAININ CATERING
Craft Service	TERRY TREBILCOCK
	ROBERT POLLACK
Extras Casting	BILL DANCE CASTING
Location Security	ON LOCATION SECURITY
Negative Cutter	SUNRISE FILM, INC.
Color Timer	MICHAEL STANWICK

Publicity	PMK, INC.
	DENNIS DAVIDSON ASSOC., INC.
Marketing	KALISH/DAVIDSON MARKETING, INC.

Production Accountant	KIMBERLY EDWARDS SHAPIRO
Assitant Accoutant	CHERYL KURK
Second Assistant Accountant	LEICIA CHAN
Additional Accounting Services	JUDY GELETKO
Post-Production Accountant	DANIELLE SOTET
Music Clearances by	EVAN M. GREENSPAN
Financing Provided by	DAIWA BANK
Completion Bond	THE COMPLETION BOND COMPANY, INC.
Legal Services	FRANKFURT, GARBUS, KLEIN & SELZ
	SINCLAIR TENENBAUM & COMPANY
Business Affairs	MEIBACH, EPSTEIN & REGIS

Titles Designed and Produced by
BALSMEYER & EVERETT

Special Thanks To:

STEVE DUNN   TESS GALLAGHER   DON BACHARDY
MARIANNE FAITHFULL   MICHAEL KIRCHBERGER   JOHN DORR
                        IRA DEUTCHMAN

TERRY ELLIS, KATE HYMAN, PAUL HUTCHINSON - IMAGO RECORDS
STEVE TROMBATORE & ALL PAYMENTS SERVICES
LUZMARIE "JELLYBEAN THE CLOWN" QUINTANA
ALICE "A. J. THE CLOWN" JONES
THOMAS BROS. MAPS ®
KIRBY VACUUMS
SHERMAN CLAY PIANOS
BOBBY PREVITE DRUMS by SLINGERLAND

"I DON'T WANT TO CRY ANYMORE"
Composed by VICTOR SCHERTZINGER
Used by permission of THE FAMOUS MUSIC
PUBLISHING COMPANIES
Performed by ANNIE ROSS and
THE LOW NOTE QUINTET

"BLUE"
Composed by JON HENDRICKS & GILDO MAHONES
Used by permission of EMI APRIL MUSIC, INC.
as Administrator for HENDRICKS MUSIC
Performed by THE LOW NOTE QUINTET
"PUNISHING KISS"
Composed by COSTELLO, MacMANUS, O'RIORDAN
Published by PLANGENT VISIONS MUSIC, LTD.
Performed by ANNIE ROSS and
THE LOW NOTE QUINTET

"TO HELL WITH LOVE"
"PRISONER OF LIFE"
"I DON'T KNOW"
Composed by DOC POMUS & MAC REBENNACK
Courtesy of STAZYBO MUSIC PUBLISHING
and SKULL MUSIC
Performed by ANNIE ROSS and
THE LOW NOTE QUINTET

"NOTHING CAN STOP ME NOW"
Composed by HORACE SILVER
Published by ECAROH MUSIC, INC./ASCAP
PUBLISHING/BMI
Performed by THE LOW QUINTET

"CONVERSATION ON A BAR STOOL"
Composed by BONO and THE EDGE
Published by POLYGRAM INTERNATIONAL
MUSIC PUBLISHING B.V.
Performed by ANNIE ROSS and
THE LOW NOTE QUINTET

"I'M GONNA GO FISHIN'"
Composed by DUKE ELLINGTON and PEGGY LEE
Published by CHAPPELL AND CO., INC./ASCAP
DENSLOW MUSIC/ASCAP
Performed by ANNIE ROSS and
THE LOW NOTE QUINTET

"FULL MOON"
Composed by DOC POMUS & MAC REBANNACK
Courtesy of STAZYBO MUSIC PUBLISHING
and SKULL MUSIC
Performed by THE LOW NOTE QUINTET
"THESE BLUES" & "THOSE BLUES"
Composed by TERRY ADAMS
Published by DOLLAR CLEF
Performed by THE LOW NOTE QUINTET

"IMITATION OF A KISS"
Composed by NATHANSON, CALE, RIBOT
Published by TABLEHEAD
Performed by THE LOW NOTE QUINTET

"CELLO CONCERTO IN D MINOR"
Composed by ANTONIN DVORAK
Performed by THE TROUT QUINTET

"CELLO CONCERTO NO. 2 OPUS 30
(FIRST MOVEMENT)"
Composed by VICTOR HERBERT
Performed by THE TROUT QUINTET

"CELLO SUITE NO. 5 IN C MINOR (BWV 1011)
Composed by JOHANN SEBASTIAN BACH
Performed by LORI SINGER

"BERCEUSE" from "THE FIREBIRD SUITE"
Composed by IGOR STRAVINSKY
Published by B. SCHOTTS SOEHNE/ASCAP
Performed by LORI SINGER

"CELLO CONCERTO NO. 2 OPUS 30
(SECOND MOVEMENT)"
Composed by VICTOR HERBERT
Performed by LORI SINGER

"SCHELOMO"
Composed by ERNEST BLOCH
Published by G. SCHIRMER, INC./ASCAP
Performed by LORI SINGER

Original Soundtrack Records released through
THE IMAGO RECORDING COMPANY
and distributed by BMG

Short Cuts by Raymond Carver
available in paperback from
VINTAGE BOOKS

DONAHUE excerpts courtesy of
MULTIMEDIA ENTERTAINMENT, INC.

HOMETIME clip courtesy of
HOMETIME VIDEO PUBLICITY, INC.

YVES ROCHER and THE COOK
courtesy of QVC NETWORK, INC.

MONSTER IN THE CLOSET clip
courtesy of TROMA

CAPTAIN PLANET AND THE PLANETEERS
clip courtesy of DIC ENTERPRISES, INC.
and TBS PRODUCTIONS, INC.

The Producers would like to thank KCAL-TV in Los Angeles for its
kind cooperation during the production of this motion picture.

Camera and Lenses by
PANAVISION

Shot on AGFA FILM

Music Recording
LE MOBILE REMOTE RECORDING STUDIOS

Re-Recording Facilities
SOUND ONE CORP.

PRODUCTION NOTES

I N 1990, director Robert Altman was flying home from Italy when he opened a book of short stories by the late Raymond Carver and was struck by his powerful prose about contemporary suburban life.

"I felt very much in tune with Carver," Altman said. "He writes about the inside . . . not the outside."

Altman is one of the world's foremost filmmakers. His most recent movie, *The Player*, set moviedom on its ear and became a major critical and commercial success throughout the world. He received the Best Director award from the New York Critics and the Cannes Film Festival for this "inside Hollywood" suspense comedy thriller that served as a metaphor for a society that places money and success above all human values.

Throughout his extraordinary career, Altman has surprised, entertained and challenged audiences with innovative films that stretch the boundaries of the medium. He has redefined the war *(M*A*S*H)*, the western *(McCabe and Mrs. Miller)*, the detective *(The Long Goodbye)* and the biographical film *(Vincent and Theo)*. He has revitalized the adaptation of plays to film *(Streamers, Fool for Love,* and *Come Back to the Five and Dime, Jimmy Dean, Jimmy Dean)* and in *Popeye* he created the first comic strip spectacular to inhabit its own stylized world.

Of all his cinematic achievements, perhaps the most inventive are the multi-charactered, multi-plotted comedic dramas *(Nashville, A Wedding, Brewster McCloud)* whose interweaving characters bridge all classes and strata of the cultural canvas. In *Tanner '88*, the award-winning mini-series in which he staged a parallel presidential campaign, *Nashville*'s political satire was extended by integrating real candidates with fictional contenders, a technique he adapted to *The Player*'s seventy celebrated cameos. In *Short Cuts*, his thirtieth film since *M*A*S*H*, *Nashville*'s character-driven tapestry expands to the frenzied, chance-driven world of Carver Country, where his characters co-exist in a perpetual recovery zone.

Short Cuts is based on nine stories and one poem by Raymond Carver, the modern prose master whose razor-sharp writing of men and women trying to cope with the working world has transformed American fiction and revived the short story. Instead of the Pacific Northwest, Altman and co-writer Frank Barhydt chose sprawling Southern California as a landscape for the film, where shooting began on July 26, 1992. The setting is the opposite of *The Player*'s Hollywood-Beverly Hills axis. Downey, Watts, Compton, Pomona, Glendale represent untapped Los Angeles, which is also Carver Country, American suburbia whose names you hear on the freeway reports but where movies rarely visit. Although the geography has changed, Carver's struggling characters face situations of emotional exposure that have struck chords of recognition in the twenty-three languages into which he has been translated.

In *Short Cuts*, Carver's people enter Altman's world in unexpected ways, interacting in tough and tender confrontations that are laced with humor and stirred by the longings which ensnare them into the next encounter.

Bringing these stories to life is a unique cast, incorporating current Hollywood favorites, legendary names and several important people from the music world. They are: Anne Archer, Bruce Davison, Robert Downey, Jr., Peter Gallagher, Buck Henry, Jennifer Jason Leigh, Jack Lemmon, Huey Lewis, Lyle Lovett, Andie MacDowell, Frances McDormand, Matthew Modine, Julianne Moore, Christopher Penn, Tim Robbins, Annie Ross, Lori Singer, Madeleine Stowe, Lili Taylor, Lily Tomlin, Tom Waits and Fred Ward.

"*Short Cuts*," critic Michael Wilmington writes, "weaves Carver's haunting tales into a multi-plotted, multi-leveled *Nashville*-style collage, an Altmanesque portrait of modern Los Angeles. In the script, which veers in mood and intention between humor, romance and horror, a collection of cops, cello players, pool cleaners, make-up artists, chauffeurs, jazz singers, phone-sex specialists, TV commentators, fishermen, waitresses and incontinent dogs, keep criss-crossing each other's paths, each unaware of the dramas unwinding on parallel track."

As poet Tess Gallagher, Carver's widow and executrix, said after reading the screenplay: "Altman doesn't do the stock thing of merely presenting Ray's scenes and characters 'as written' in the stories—he instead causes surprising turns to happen, improvising from original material as a jazz musician might . . . He's engaged Ray's stories on a very deep and innovative level."

And producer Cary Brokaw says: "*Short Cuts* reveals a great filmmaker at the peak of his powers."

Altman feels "There is no right way or wrong way. *Short Cuts* and Carver are about two sides to everything. Something happens to one person, but what if the opposite happened, what would their behavior be like? One person is lucky, another is unlucky. That's what this whole thing is about."

At sixty-eight, when most directors are near retirement or have finally achieved a comfortable pattern in their work, Altman has made an epic tragic-comedy of morals that is arguably the most bold and daring film of his career.

It is a major work to be reckoned with, from a constantly evolving film-maker, who continues to challenge himself and us.

—MICHAEL KAPLAN
Associate Producer of *Short Cuts*

STILLS

THE RANGE of intensity and inner projection in these Don Bachardy portraits of the *Short Cuts* cast, director, co-writer and of myself, reflect his success at complete identification with his subjects. "I had a sense of painting them from the inside, almost as if I were painting self-portraits."

A metamorphosis does actually seem to take place. Indeed, while one sits for him, Bachardy's face passes through swift, bird-like dartings of alertness, much pursing of the mouth, twitchings of the cheek and brow. "I'm trying to physically feel like my sitter. Making faces with my own face. It probably looks to my sitter as if I'm demented."

Bachardy's biggest challenge is always whether or not a person will be able to sit still and concentrate for the entire four-hour session. Two portraits were done at each sitting, and the only respite from stillness came when the actor initiated the pose for the second portrait. "One sitter got hungry and simply disappeared for an hour and a half in the middle of the session. I didn't know if he was coming back."

But for most of the twenty-two actors, as they sat in the costumes of the characters they portrayed, it was a trance-like encounter with their own bodies, the challenge to stay attentive and still at the same time. "One never in a lifetime ever does sit that still for that long," Bachardy says in appreciation of the help and participation his best sitters give him.

He always begins with the eyes. "If the eyes are wrong you've really lost it." Since he feels the identity of the sitter comes most through the eyes, he must paint them at the height of the vitality of the subject, as the session begins. The pressure of his medium—fast drying acrylic on paper, plus the variable of his sitters' temperaments, and the stricture of a time limit—seems to stimulate his creativity as much as it threatens his resourcefulness in the moment. He says he has been particularly aware in this series of reaching through the costumed performer to the person inside, letting that shine through.

143

Bachardy did have the luxury of becoming visually familiar with the actors in "dailies" as they performed two or three days prior to their coming to sit. Their costumes would be delivered to this studio the night before, and they would slip into them to prepare for the session. In the best portraits one senses a trust and opening into time as each subject surrenders their dishevelled gazings from a raft of stillness.

The effort to give the body its "thingness" is of itself compelling in these caricature-like abrasions of the real. In each portrait the sitter takes on their own likeness in the darting gestures of the painter. Soon they are flying with him into the whole of silence and space with his candid strokings, tenacious slashings of color, delicate bees of frank testimony, cagey beauty—the chipped, still-wet transparencies by which he's entered at their eyes and opened with them somewhere entirely unexpected, between fixity and vertigo.

These stripped-down essences by Bachardy impress me as being miraculously paired with the fusion of Altman-Carver. They exude power, loneliness and solitude. They grimace, brood, evade, confront and dream. They shiver with aliveness, the way a hallway mirror pulses into fractured light and bewildered shards of human form, the moment you open the door and step into entryway. Each of these portraits is an entry left boldly open for us by this extraordinary artist.

—TESS GALLAGHER

April 15, 1993
Port Angeles, Washington